ALSO BY KATHRYN REED

*Sleeping with Strangers:
An Airbnb Host's Life in Lake Tahoe and Mexico*

Snowshoeing Around Lake Tahoe: Must-Do Scenic Treks

The Dirt Around Lake Tahoe: Must-Do Scenic Hikes

Lake Tahoe Trails For All Seasons

MUST-DO HIKING AND SNOWSHOE TREKS

KATHRYN REED

Lake Tahoe Trails For All Seasons: Must-Do Hiking and Snowshoe Treks by Kathryn Reed. Published by Kathryn Reed
P.O Box 853, Chico, CA 95927
www.KathrynReed.com
© 2020 Kathryn Reed.
All rights reserved. No part of this book may be reproduced or transmitted in any form or by any means, electronic, mechanical, photocopying, recording, or otherwise, without prior written permission. For permissions contact:
kr@kathrynreed.com
Library of Congress Control Number: 2020904851
ISBN: 978-1-952003-04-2
Front and back cover, and interior photos © Kathryn Reed.
Author photo © Tim Parsons.
Cover design by Ponderosa Pine Design.

Contents

Acknowledgments i
Introduction ii

South Shore/American River Canyon

HIKING

Ralston Peak 2
Rubicon Trail 4
Mount Tallac 6
Lake Aloha 8
Horsetail Falls 10
Star Lake 12
Eagle Lake, Eagle Falls 14
Angora Burn Area 16
Dardanelles Lake 18
Angora Lakes 20
Roundabout at Heavenly 22
Twin Lakes 23
Angora Ridge 25
Twin Peaks 27
Tallac Site 29
Lam Watah Trail 31
Pony Express Trail 33
Hawley Grade Falls 35
Cascade Falls 37

SNOWSHOEING

Roundabout at Heavenly 40
Becker Peak 42
Emerald Bay 44
Fallen Leaf Lake 46
Tallac Site 48
Baldwin Beach 50

Contents

Maggie's Peak 52
Van Sickle Bi-State Park 54
Angora Ridge 56
Echo Lake Ridge 58
Twin Peaks 60
Emerald Bay Campground 62
High Meadow 64
Grass Lake 66
Lake Tahoe Golf Course 68

West Shore

HIKING
Eagle Rock 72
Ellis Peak 74
Homewood Mountain Resort 76
Tahoe-Yosemite Trail 78
Twin Peaks 80

SNOWSHOEING
Sugar Pine Point 84

North Shore/Truckee

HIKING
5 Lakes 88
Palisades Tahoe 90
Page Meadow 92
Top of Palisades Tahoe's Tram 94
Donner Lake 96

East Shore

HIKING
Marlette Lake 100
Snow Valley Peak 102
Galena Creek Waterfall 104

Contents

TRT at Spooner Summit 106
Prey Meadows 109
Spooner Lake 111

SNOWSHOEING

Marlette Lake 114
Skunk Harbor 116

Alpine County

HIKING

Showers Lake 120
Winnemucca Lake 122
Raymond Lake 124
Granite Lake 127
Meiss Meadow 129
Markleeville Waterfall 131
Charity Valley 133
Curtz and Summit Lakes 135

SNOWSHOEING

Elephants Back 138
Carson Pass 140
Hope Valley 142

Carson Valley/Carson City/Reno

HIKING

Jones Creek Trails 146
Genoa Falls 148
Prison Hill 150
Pine Nuts 152
Fay-Luther Trails 154
Carson River 156

Acknowledgments

I will always be grateful to my parents for taking me to Lake Tahoe as a child, first in winter and then in summer. They introduced me to the outdoors in various forms — camping, water skiing, hiking, snow skiing. My mom became a snowshoer after I moved to Lake Tahoe, making many outings even more special. She has also been on many of these hikes.

I have always found hiking and snowshoeing to be more enjoyable with friends. Thank you to all my trail partners.

Sue Wood, Rosemary Manning and Donna Rockwood were on many of these excursions. They helped rate the treks in terms of scenic quality and challenge.

Thank you to Vicky Shea for the cover design. Joann Eisenbrandt was diligent with getting this into print. Several people offered advice as the book came together — thank you.

To all the supporters of *Lake Tahoe News*, who for nine years were part of my daily life in some form and who first inspired me to write these stories, thank you.

Introduction

Lake Tahoe is a year-round playground for outdoor lovers. This guidebook will keep you hiking or snowshoeing every month of the year. While both activities are good exercise, even better is getting into nature, being immersed in her beauty, and venturing places not everyone has gone.

Lake Tahoe Trails For All Seasons: Must-Do Hiking and Snowshoe Treks is for everyone who likes to play in the greater Lake Tahoe area whether it's on a dirt path or a snowy trail. These hikes and snowshoe treks were originally written for *Lake Tahoe News*, the preeminent news source at the time. They were all written by me, an average athlete. The stories have been revised to make sense for readers who live in and outside the Lake Tahoe Basin.

This isn't your traditional guidebook because it's written in narrative form. Each excursion is a story unto itself. Some have historical references, others describe the landscape, while all include details unique to that particular outing. Four people provided input on the "challenge" and "scenic" ratings in the book. This is something that was not included with the original *LTN* stories.

Two of the best things about hiking and snowshoeing are that it usually doesn't cost to do either sport, and most everyone can do the activity. Even so, be sure to carry cash because a use or parking fee is being implemented at more trailheads.

Many of the winter excursions can be done on snowshoes or cross country skis. It will depend on your ability level. I say if you can walk, you can snowshoe. Your gait is just a little wider. Snow conditions will be a factor in considering the challenge. There is a big difference between having to break trail and someone having beaten you to it.

Another added challenge for hiking and snowshoeing can be the elevation; both at the starting point as well as the maximum level you will hit. Living at sea level may make some of these excursions seem a bit harder.

Be smart when you play outside. Take more water than you think you will need. It's easy to become dehydrated — even in winter. This is because the cooler temperature and less sweating may make you forget to drink. Take extra clothing, food and a first aid kit on all excursions. Whatever you pack in, be sure to pack out. Don't expect your cell phone to work in the wilderness. It can be a good idea to let someone know when you expect to return so help can be summoned if you are overdue.

Know if dogs are allowed, and if you need water for them or if enough will be supplied by streams and lakes. Water sources may be frozen in winter, and not all dogs eat snow. Plowing through powder will be more exhausting for a dog. Short-haired dogs may need a coat. At various times be sure to check their paws for snow accumulation.

Take pictures, but leave everything else as you found it.

Time to lace up those boots.

Kathryn Reed

South Shore/ American River Canyon Hikes

"Of all the paths you can take in life,
make sure a few of them are dirt."

— *John Muir*

Ralston Peak: 360 Degrees Of Awe

Scenic: 10
Challenge: 8
Special note: Call to make sure the Echo Lake boat taxi is operating; bring cash.
Getting there: From South Lake Tahoe, take Highway 50 west. A short distance after cresting Echo Summit, turn right onto Johnson Pass Road. Stay to the left. The narrow road leads to Echo Lake.

Mount Tallac is the icon of Lake Tahoe's South Shore, but that grandeur pales in comparison to the razzle-dazzle Mother Nature provides from the top of Ralston Peak.

From that vantage point it is Tallac's backside that hikers see.

The summit of Ralston is so much better than being at the top of Tallac because the vistas are jaw-dropping gorgeous. Civilization is nowhere on the horizon unless ski slopes count.

It was odd feeling like I was in the middle of nowhere and yet knowing exactly where I was. Familiar landmarks surrounded me as I took in the 360-degree view: barren runs of Sierra-at-Tahoe; splotches of snow dotting Pyramid Peak, which at 9,983 feet is the highest mountain in the Crystal Range and Desolation Wilderness; the pools of Lake Aloha that resemble a moonscape; Price, Jack and Dick's peaks looking manageable to climb from our perch at 9,235 feet; Lake Tahoe so vast it could be the ocean; Fallen Leaf Lake so small it could be Heather Lake.

With 50-mph winds forecast for our destination, we were dressed more like a winter hike than summer. Warmth was not what we found in late June, but that didn't matter, except it meant the 12 women and two dogs didn't linger long.

This landmark can be seen from Highway 50 near Horsetail Falls. While there are several routes to get to the top, we started at Echo Lake.

We cut off 2 miles each way by taking the boat across. (Our trek was 8 miles round trip.) The ride is beautiful. The path starts out rocky. The runners in the group sprinted to the lead. Others fell to the back, taking in the scenery of Tamarack Lake, which comes up on the left.

There were lupine, phlox, pussy paws, wallflower, Indian paintbrush, shooting star and sulphur buckwheat to photograph. At this elevation the wildflowers were smaller than what is found at lake level – dwarf-like.

Winter's sparse snowfall had turned western-facing manzanita black. Lack of water will kill these bushes in the backcountry. While they are a species that burns hot in a fire, dead manzanita is more susceptible to fire than a live plant. Fire is more of a concern for the manzanita trees because it becomes a ladder fuel.

Trail signs pop up, indicating so many choices for where to play in Desolation Wilderness. Some of the routes are along the Pacific Crest Trail.

We took the second left headed toward Lake of the Woods. We kept her to our right, never reaching her shore. Pyramid Peak, aptly named because it looks like pharaohs could call this mountain home, looms over this lake.

Pockets of snow cropped up, but nothing substantial enough to hinder our progress. We traipsed through a soggy meadow before the last ascent to the tip-top. Mountain hemlock and white bark pine sprouted from the rugged terrain. They like it at this elevation.

Giddy with the delight of summiting Ralston Peak, we were all smiles while taking in the scenery and feeling like we were on top of the world.

Rubicon Trail: 50 Shades Of Blue

Scenic: 9
Challenge: 5
Special note: Best early season hike in the Lake Tahoe Basin.
Getting there: From South Lake Tahoe, take Highway 89 north, through the hairpin turns, around Emerald Bay and park in the Vikingsholm lot on the right. Go down the paved trail toward the castle. Before reaching the castle, the Rubicon Trail is to the left.

It says something about a trail when, after being on it multiple times, the camera still comes out and the oohs and ahhs are endless.

That's the thing about the Rubicon Trail; it never gets old. It connects Emerald Bay State Park to D.L. Bliss State Park.

It's all about the scenery.

We were in awe of the endless hues of blue and the depths to which we could see the floor of Lake Tahoe. It was calm on this particular day. The lake looked inviting, but we didn't even want to dip our toes because we knew how cold it was.

A motorboat went along the shore, while kayakers were in Emerald Bay.

A treat was discovering an osprey's nest. With binoculars we could see there was movement in the nest perched on top of a dead tree.

The odd-looking snow plant was out. Otherwise, not much colorful flora is along this trail. This hike is all about the water.

It's a great early-season trek, especially in heavy snow years, because it is at lake level. Plus, there are no crowds. Before summer, no one is in the boat-in campground.

It's not a difficult hike, but there also aren't a ton of places to take a break. Much of the route is flat, though there are spots with slight undulations.

Closer to the D.L. Bliss side is an offshoot trail to an old lighthouse. The Rubicon Point Lighthouse is the second highest elevation lighthouse in the United States.

This can be a round-trip trek starting at either state park or a one-way if a car is left at each park. It's a mile down from the Vikingsholm parking lot to the trailhead, then 4.5 miles along the water's edge. If D.L. Bliss is not open, it's a 2-mile climb from the beach to the vehicle you dropped if you make this a one-way excursion.

It costs to park at each state park. Some free parking can be found near Eagle Falls on the other side of Highway 89.

Dogs are not allowed.

Mount Tallac:
An Icon Worth Conquering

Scenic: 8
Challenge: 8
Special note: There is more than one starting point.
Getting there: From South Lake Tahoe, take Highway 89 north. Turn left on Fallen Leaf Lake Road. Weave around to where it dead-ends at the trailhead.

As the sky was getting light, we could see our destination just a few steps away. We had made it in time to meet our goal.

It was the best sunrise I have ever seen.

Sitting atop Mount Tallac at 9,735 feet as the sun comes over the mountains and shines all her glory onto Lake Tahoe is something to behold. Pictures don't adequately capture all the hues Mother Nature paints across the sky.

The wispy clouds seemed liked jewels — necklaces and bracelets to accessorize the spectacle unfolding before us.

What a birthday gift.

I wanted to do something memorable for my 50th birthday that was Tahoe-centric. Climbing Mount Tallac under a full moon and being at the peak for sunrise are two things I had thought about doing for some time. Why not do both in one hike? My birthday weekend in September happened to be a full moon. Perfect.

I invited a few friends to make the trek with me. Two took me up on the adventure. Darla, who I've known since third grade, came up from the San Francisco Bay Area, and Kele, a friend since we were in our 20s working in Tahoe, came down from Oregon. We left the house about 1 a.m.; we were hiking 30 minutes later.

It was a good thing we all had headlamps because the full moon was not of much assistance. The trees were in the way of that natural light. The moon eventually set and we were left in total darkness. At times we shut off our lights to be dazzled by the Milky Way. This was a show unto itself. Most people only see something like this in a planetarium. This truly was magical with zero ambient light.

Big spiders, several of them, were the main wildlife out at this hour. For whatever reason, they were right on the trail. (They didn't look like friends of Charlotte's, but we still let them be.)

To say everything looks different in the dark is stating the obvious. Thank goodness for trail markers, otherwise who knows where we would have ended up. It was only near Gilmore Lake that we were unsure of the route. We figured it out on the second attempt.

We had started at the Glen Alpine Springs Trailhead, the least steep of the routes. It is, however, the longest at about 12 miles round trip. We thought it wiser to go the easier route in the dark.

The summit, well, it's one of those special places that can touch one's soul. For many reasons it was more magical this time. It was so wonderful that there were only four other people up there. (At other times it can be congested, with people yakking on their cell phones.) They were celebrating a 25th birthday and thought it was cool 50-year-olds were doing the same thing.

And while they briefly made me feel my age, we proved age has a thing on youth. We shared our hand warmers with them (they weren't prepared for the cold) and we were the ones with Prosecco to toast the occasion.

It was a toast to Tahoe, friendship, a great 50 years and a future of unknown possibilities.

Lake Aloha: Like Something Out Of This World

Scenic: 7
Challenge: 8
Special note: Booties are a good idea for dogs.
Getting there: From South Lake Tahoe, go north on Highway 89. Turn left on Fallen Leaf Lake Road. Wind around and park at the Glen Alpine Trailhead. Once on the trail, follow signs for Susie Lake and Lake Aloha.

Susie and Heather lakes were the only ones we were supposed to meet along the way. However, in early spring there was so much snowmelt that pools of water looked like new lakes. This is not an exaggeration.

Water was everywhere. I expected the Glen Alpine Springs area to be a bit flooded, but it wasn't bad. It was as we climbed that we came across these foreign water bodies.

Looming walls of granite appeared to be weeping as water seemed to stain the light gray rock.

Waterfalls not ordinarily running in the summer looked like a spigot had been turned on.

It's an interesting dichotomy. On the one hand there was so much water that it would be hard to know California was in a major drought. On the other hand, the runoff should not have been so substantive; the moisture should have been in the form of snow.

In several places, it was necessary to walk across logs or hop from rock to rock to cross the running water.

Donna and I made the 12-mile round-trip trek to Lake Aloha in May. This picturesque lake in Desolation Wilderness should have tons of snow on the trail. Not so. The couple snowfields we traversed were no big deal.

Really, we shouldn't have been able to be there. It was too early in the season to be on this route without snowshoes. It's doubtful I would be on it in winter because Fallen Leaf Lake Road is usually closed, and the route has no markers for winter recreationists.

I learned this is the time to make this ascent. One of the fabulous things about this hike in the early season is the lack of people on the trail. With this being one of the portals to Mount Tallac, there is often a bevy of foot traffic that can make it seem like anything but a wilderness area.

A few backpackers were coming and going. On this particular day I was glad it was a day trip for us. It was too windy and cold to spend much time at this lake, which looks like it's from another world. We are reminded of the time of year by the snow lining the shore on the other side of the lake, which then extends to peaks that seem to scratch the sky. Mount Pierce and Pyramid Peak are the most visible from this vantage point.

This granite basin has only a few trees protruding from the edges of the water. Rock is the dominant feature — including the islands.

I had forgotten how much granite there is on this trek; much more rock than dirt.

Starting out at the trailhead we were at 6,560 feet. Lake Aloha is 8,170 feet.

Horsetail Falls: Worth Seeing Up Close

Scenic: 7
Challenge: 8
Special note: Parking spaces fill fast, so go early — or don't go on a weekend.
Getting there: From South Lake Tahoe, take Highway 50 west toward Placerville. The trailhead is outside the Lake Tahoe Basin. Parking is on the right at Pyramid Creek. There is a fee to park, so bring cash.

From a distance, especially driving west on Highway 50, the falls look like a horse's tail, thus the name Horsetail Falls. It's one of the most spectacular waterfalls in the area, from afar and close up.

This is one of those destinations where the end can be anywhere one chooses because there are so many scenic vistas along the way.

There is a designated loop. While pretty, it doesn't go to the falls. There also isn't a sign saying when to get off this section of trail.

Pyramid Creek is the early focal point. Downstream this water eventually ends up in the American River.

At times the trail is not well defined. Our group of 12 took a couple U-turns and crossed the creek before we finally found our way to the end point we had all agreed on. There we sat on slabs of granite eating our lunch, watching the water descend in all its glory. Absolutely stunning.

The water tumbling down comes from Lake Aloha. It's possible to hike there and to other lakes in Desolation Wilderness from this point. This is only recommended for more advanced hikers.

Almost every year at least one person is seriously hurt or dies in this area because of climbing beyond his or her ability level, not respecting how cold the water is or the swiftness of the current.

Our trek was about 4 miles round trip.

With so much granite, it is a good idea to have booties for dogs.

Star Lake:
A Shimmering Jewel

Scenic: 7
Challenge: 7
Special note: Go early in the day.
Getting there: From South Lake Tahoe, turn onto Al Tahoe Boulevard. Go right on Pioneer Trail. Turn left onto High Meadow Drive. (Sierra House Elementary School is on the corner.) Drive as far as you can. Take the main trail that looks like a road.

"Are we there yet?" is never a good question because inevitably the answer is "no," and the destination is still far away.

Such was the case with the hike to Star Lake. High Meadow Trailhead is up, straight up, no switchbacks, on an old pitted road that is more suitable for a four-wheel drive vehicle than for legs.

Enduring this stretch of trail, though, was well worth it. Star Lake is a jewel in the Sierra. As Rosemary said, it must have gotten its name from being so high, as if stars would be within reach at nightfall.

The lake is at 9,100 feet.

Carolyn, who was wearing her Fitbit, recorded 35,375 steps for the entire hike. That included walking around her house that morning, as well as having logged 14.53 miles on the trail.

Before reaching High Meadow, we turned off to the right toward Star Lake. (There is a sign.) The trail became single-track, more gradual and even level at times, with the lodgepole and Jeffrey pines being interspersed with some juniper trees higher up. At one point the five of us walked through a quartz field; not a common sight in Tahoe.

Intermittent views of Lake Tahoe and the entire South Shore unfolded below us.

Water flowed in a couple spots, which AJ my dog was appreciative of.

Our destination, Star Lake, was too cold for our gang to swim in, but that didn't stop others from cooling off. A couple tents were in the area, with openings to views of the jagged mountains surrounding the lake. Plenty of beach-like areas surround the water, perfect for a lunch break.

Monument Peak, at the backside of Heavenly Mountain Resort, is on one side of the meadow at 10,067 feet. The meadow itself is at an elevation of 7,834 feet. Across the other side of the meadow are Freel, Jobs and Jobs Sister.

We were able to make a loop to avoid the road on the way back. We turned right toward the meadow on our way out. In 2012, the U.S. Forest Service completed a three-year, $2 million restoration of the meadow that realigned Cold Creek to more of its natural meander.

The foliage is denser and lush along the Cold Creek Trail, with aspens that in fall would be spectacular. This is so much prettier than the road we went up on in the morning. It's also longer, but well worth it.

Multiple trails are in the area, including the Tahoe Rim Trail. It's popular with mountain bikers, but one needs to be in good shape and able to navigate challenging terrain. The Monument Pass Trail was completed in 2014, and connects High Meadow to the Tahoe Rim Trail at Monument Pass. The Star Lake Trail was completed in 2012 and was rerouted from the original road.

There were more "Are we there yets?" on the way down, but no one was complaining about having spent another glorious day hiking in Lake Tahoe.

Eagle Lake, Eagle Falls: Easy Enough For The Family

Scenic: 7
Challenge: 5
Special note: The U.S. Forest Service charges a fee to park.
Getting there: From South Lake Tahoe, go north on Highway 89. The Eagle Falls parking area is on the left at the end of Emerald Bay, before reaching the parking area for Vikingsholm. If going to Eagle Lake, fill out the permit for Desolation Wilderness.

Water. In June it's often the common denominator for all hikes in and around the Lake Tahoe area. That's a good thing when waterfalls are involved.

Rumbling water is a constant sound on the trek from the Eagle Falls parking lot to Eagle Lake. Sometimes it's roaring, sometimes a bit fainter, but always there.

This area was revamped in 2005 with a walkway from Highway 89 to the trailhead, which means no longer having to contend with vehicles to get to the path. Restrooms were put in at the same time.

Our destination was the upper falls and then Eagle Lake. The Forest Service website says it's a 20-minute, 1-mile walk to the lake. With all the Kodak moments along the way, we took at least twice that long. For those wanting a longer hike, a sign clearly states when to turn left to reach the three Velmas, Dicks, and Fontanillis lakes.

Starting off we took the loop to the right, which is longer than going directly to the upper falls. We didn't care. It was about enjoying the scenery.

It's one of those magical places that even the most jaded person would have to pause to appreciate Mother Nature's handiwork.

Interpretive signs are on this section. I learned something: Emerald Bay is 3 miles long and 1 mile wide.

Water was on the trail, making it a good idea to wear hiking boots.

Spanning Upper Eagle Falls is a bridge. Water rushed beneath me. It was hard to hear my own thoughts because of the thundering falls. Doing a 360, I marveled at the granite above me, the amount of water running on either side, the rocks being pounded by the snowmelt.

To do the loop, the bridge is where you'd turn around. But we weren't done.

Across the bridge we hit snow. Mostly it was dirt the rest of the way, but that white stuff was unavoidable at times.

Some winters, so much snow causes waterfalls to spill from the sides of the mountain as if spigots have opened. A sheet of granite can look like a streak of tears.

Granite is more dominate in this section of Desolation Wilderness than conifers. Spires of jagged rock line one wall of what feels like a canyon at times.

We stopped for lunch before reaching the lake. Slabs of smooth granite beckoned us to recline, until an aggressive chipmunk smelled our food. He reminded me of the "friendly" critters atop Mount Tallac.

Emerald Bay and Lake Tahoe are in the distance.

Onward we went to the lake. It looked beautiful, but so uninviting. I wouldn't even dip my toe in her frigid waters. On a hot summer day people swim and paddle out to the little island. No one was doing so this day … we were all still trying to have traction on slick snow.

Angora Burn Area: Multiple Trails

Scenic: 7
Challenge: 3
Special note: Good for families.
Getting there: From South Lake Tahoe, continue on Lake Tahoe Boulevard at the Y. Turn right on Tahoe Mountain Road. Park at the third green gate. Not all the trails are marked.

The dictionary definition of a forest is "a large area covered chiefly with trees and undergrowth." It's hard to know what to call a former forest that is covered with undergrowth and what looks like poles.

This is Tahoe Mountain after the 2007 Angora Fire.

The trees, such as they are, are like large salt and pepper shakers. It burned so hot, what was once brown and green trees are no more. "Stumps" are taller than me. These trees' lives were taken too soon, all because negligent people failed to put out an illegal campfire at Seneca Pond.

When it comes to forest devastation, Angora's 3,000-plus acres are a blip on the map, especially when compared to the fires that have burned throughout California since then. It was the loss of 254 houses that was the most impactful.

Among the standing dead trees is an understory of life. However, much of it is invasive and flammable like white thorn and bull thistle. Grass can be a couple feet tall.

This is U.S. Forest Service land. The agency says it is normal for this type of flora to grow after a fire because these species like disturbed soils. The Forest Service has treated some areas to kill the invasive flora. Summer rains help the vegetation grow.

The U.S. Forest Service says this flash fuel would burn quickly, but at a low intensity if a fire were to come through the area again. Even in windy conditions this type of fuel is easy to suppress, according to the federal agency. Some of this vegetation is along the trails off Tahoe Mountain Road, and some is near houses.

A map at the third gate on the right on Tahoe Mountain Road shows a variety of trails mostly used by mountain bikers. They are also good for dog walks, and evidence showed equestrians use them as well. With so many options, mileage will vary.

The views are fabulous. The South Shore peaks (Tallac, Jobs, Freel), Lake Tahoe from the ridge, and even the developed area are interesting from this perspective.

Dardanelles Lake: Bedazzling Beauty

Scenic: 6
Challenge: 6
Special note: At age 76 my mom said, "It's a wee bit more than a moderate hike."
Getting there: From South Lake Tahoe, go west on Highway 50. In Meyers, be in the left lane in the roundabout, taking the second exit onto Highway 89. Before reaching the summit of Luther Pass, Big Meadow Trailhead parking is on the left. Park. The trail starts on the other side of the highway. You passed the trailhead marker on Highway 89 on your right. Follow the signs to Dardanelles Lake. Signage is good for the most part. However, about a quarter mile from the sign that has you go right, you need to make a sharp left. The trail is obvious, but it splits, also going straight, so it's not obvious that turning left leads to Dardanelles.

Pretty face, cow parsnips, California valerian, forget-me-nots, lupine, columbine, Indian paintbrush, larkspur, groundsel – these are just some of the flowers that flourish in a kaleidoscope of color along the trail to Dardanelles Lake.

It's helpful to have someone on the trail telling you what you're looking at instead of just saying — ooh, look at that pretty red or yellow or purple flower. They actually have names.

This splash of color can be an added bonus to the hike. I don't often think of this trail as a wildflower destination, but instead I like it for the magical alpine lake at the end of the 3.5 miles.

When there has been an abundance of moisture, not only are

the flowers prolific, so are the mosquitoes. Even with bug juice, we had plenty of itchy souvenirs.

Another consequence of the snowfall and water is that the bridge leading into Big Meadow can collapse. But that's not the only water crossing. Fairly stable rocks have been strategically placed in other sections to make stream crossings doable.

It can be magical to see the array of wildflowers. Some were so tiny, others were like groundcover, while a few grew higher than my knees. I wanted to pick them to create a bouquet, but instead I only took their pictures.

Big Meadow is aptly named. The tall grasses made me channel Julie Andrews, but I didn't sing out loud. The hills really did seem alive.

We carried on. After all, the meadow is just the beginning.

Plenty of welcome shade covered the trail. Mostly it's dirt all along a moderate climb. We started at 7,200 feet, with the maximum elevation being 7,760 feet. The worst part is leaving the lake. It's a good descent at the end to Dardanelles Lake, so climbing out is no fun. We certainly didn't appreciate the downhill enough, as we were whining going out.

Oh, but that lake. It shimmers in a way that makes it look like it's dancing. Granite walls line one side. It's possible to swim to the rocks.

Flat granite provided an ideal spot for lunch. While there were several people doing the same, we still had our own spot in the Sierra.

Color on this trail is not limited to the wildflowers. In the fall, the aspens come alive in their array of yellows and oranges.

Angora Lakes: Hike And Then Swim

Scenic: 6
Challenge: 6
Special note: Order a lemonade.
Getting there: From South Lake Tahoe, at the Y go straight on Lake Tahoe Boulevard toward South Tahoe High School or the burn area. Turn right on Tahoe Mountain Road. Go right at the T intersection. Go left at the next T. The road curves a bit. Go slow. In the summer and through early October the U.S. Forest Service gate on the left is open. Park nearby to get the full hike. Drive up the road for a half-mile hike from the parking lot to the resort. It costs to park at the resort.

Hiking to Angora Lakes is one of those mixed blessings in the heart of summer. The route is crowded with vehicles on what is really a one-lane road; however, the end result is a majestic alpine wonder.

It's one of those 3-mile climbs I never get tired of no matter the season.

Plus, Angora Road is multipurpose — good for walking, biking, snowshoeing and cross country skiing. In the fall, the aspens at the start of the route are stunning. In winter it feels so much more like being in the wilderness, even somewhat desolate.

It got its name from the angora goats that used to graze in the area.

While we called it a hike, it's hard to do so when the bulk of the walk is on pavement.

It's not the best excursion for dogs because they are not allowed to swim in the upper lake where all the people are, which is the easiest point to reach the water. However, there were no signs at the lower lake saying dogs were not permitted. So, AJ and Buddy were able to get a little swim in and some water there. There is no other water along this trail for dogs to cool off in.

Still, what makes this a good people destination are the views and the ability to walk next to each other.

After a fairly steady ascent, the road flattens out on Angora Ridge. To the left is the Angora burn area. Tons of underbrush gives the hillside a look of rejuvenation, though the blackened and ash white remnants of dead trees from the 2007 fire dominate the landscape. To the right is serene Fallen Leaf Lake. Beyond it is Lake Tahoe.

From the parking lot, the trail is dirt for about one-half mile. This allows the experience to be called a hike.

Food may be purchased in the little store, while paddleboards and kayaks are available for rent.

For those who want to spend more than a day or afternoon at Angora Lakes, there are nine cabins that rent on a weekly basis. The Hildinger family has been operating the seasonal resort on U.S. Forest Service land since 1917.

Roundabout: Ski Slope Harder In Hiking Boots

Scenic: 6
Challenge: 6
Special note: Take lots of water; much of the trail is exposed.
Getting there: From South Lake Tahoe, turn onto Ski Run Boulevard. Turn left on Needle Peak Road, right on Wildwood Avenue, left on Saddle Road, right on Keller Road, then right on Sherman Way. The road dead-ends at Sherman. There is a gate there. Start walking.

Skiing down Roundabout run is about as easy as it gets at Heavenly Mountain Resort.

Hiking or biking up it when the snow is long gone is another story. Suddenly the terrain seems steep in places. It is definitely not a green route in this direction.

It's not that the 5-plus-mile hike is super strenuous, it's just that it keeps going up. Most trails around the South Shore have a more gradual grade, with some straightaways, and even a descent along the way. Not so with this trek.

Being on any ski trail without snow is always disconcerting for the skier/snowboarder because things don't look the same. Warmer weather also allows time to linger and enjoy the views, not needing to have fingers turn blue while taking pictures.

The top of Patsy's reports the elevation at 8,290 feet. Another hundred feet or so and Lake Tahoe sprawls beyond the Gunbarrel run. The Stateline casinos, Edgewood Tahoe Golf Course and Nevada Beach are off to the right in Nevada. In the other direction are Ski Run Marina, Tahoe Keys and Camp Richardson — all in California.

Twin Lakes: Worth The Drive To The Trailhead

Scenic: 6
Challenge: 5
Special note: Plenty of water for four-legged hikers. It costs to park.
Getting there: From South Lake Tahoe, take Highway 50 west for 20.7 miles to Wrights Lake Road. Turn right. Follow signs for Twin and Grouse lakes. After 8.8 miles there is a big parking lot. The trailhead begins just below the parking lot.

We almost didn't make it to the lake. There were so many pretty places along the stream that called out to us it was hard not to stop to take it all in.

It was one of those hikes where the journey truly surpassed the destination. And the destination was stunning, especially with the multi-legged waterfall in the distance cascading down the granite wall.

While there were some wildflowers along the route, this excursion is more about the water.

The end point was Twin Lakes in Desolation Wilderness.

Round trip it's 6 miles, though we did a little loop at the end that took us closer to Wrights Lake to make it more like a 7-mile day.

Starting out the terrain is lush. The tree canopy provided a shady route. This was where the bulk of the flowers were.

The climb is gradual, though there are some granite steps that might make those with knee issues want poles.

Dirt gave way to granite. In some ways this was reminiscent of hiking to Horsetail Falls. However, there wasn't so much rock that AJ needed her booties to protect her paws.

What's better about this trail compared to Horsetail is that people have outlined with rocks where to go, or they built cairns. The markers are definitely needed at various locations.

While Twin Lakes looked inviting, the temperature was icy. The wind made it necessary to put the layer back on that was removed on the way up.

Coming down, Wrights Lake, essentially the starting point, looked so tiny and far away. With starting at about 7,000 feet and going up nearly 1,300 feet, the expanse below is vast.

Angora Ridge: Dirt Trail A Good Alternative

Scenic: 6
Challenge: 4
Special note: No water for dogs.
Getting there: From South Lake Tahoe, at the Y go straight on Lake Tahoe Boulevard. Turn right on Tahoe Mountain Road. Go right at the T intersection. Go left at the next T. The road curves a bit. Go slow. Additional parking has been created near Angora Lake Road. The trail starts to the right of the Angora gate/road.

Hiking Angora Ridge is better now thanks to a bunch of mountain bikers and the U.S. Forest Service.

No longer do people have to contend with vehicles or be on pavement to reach Angora Ridge.

The nonprofit Tahoe Area Mountain Biking Association partnered with the federal land owner to build a trail that basically parallels the road. One of the best parts is the road is not visible much of the time.

While this was built as a single-track mountain bike route, plenty of hikers (some with dogs) also enjoy this route. It goes from where Tahoe Mountain Road intersects with Angora Lakes Road and comes out near the fire lookout. That's as far as we went that day. A short way up the paved road the dirt trail resumes to the right. It ends at the parking lot below the resort. The full trail is about 3 miles one way, with the lookout about halfway.

It doesn't take long before Fallen Leaf Lake comes into view. Be sure to turn around to see Lake Tahoe as well. Mount Tallac becomes quite a presence as well.

This is what makes this trail so much more scenic than being on the road – the views are stunning most of the way. You don't have to wait to hit the ridge to get them, which is the case with the road.

Seeing the houses on Tahoe Mountain was something I had never noticed from the road.

Being on foot gave me a chance to survey the route to see if I'd want to come back on my bike. Seeing people pushing their bikes oddly made me want to try it. I didn't want to be the only one possibly not pedaling. It didn't look technical, just steep (for a bike, not on foot) in places. Families were out, both on bikes and walking.

The cyclists can be coming down pretty fast, but all were courteous as we scampered to get out of their way.

It took about 2,000 hours of volunteer labor and thousands of dollars in private donations to make the nearly 5 miles of trail in this area a reality. There is also a connector from the Angora burn area.

More trails are on the drawing board, including extending the Angora trail north to connect with Fallen Leaf Lake.

The ultimate goal is to have a mountain bike trail that goes around Lake Tahoe. Yes, there is the 165-mile Tahoe Rim Trail, but that is for hikers and much of it is off-limits to bikes.

Twin Peaks:
A Pair Of Beauties

Scenic: 6
Challenge: 4
Special note: A great in-town hike.
Getting there: From the Y in South Lake Tahoe, continue on Lake Tahoe Boulevard. Turn left on Sawmill Road. Park immediately in the lot to the left.

Summiting several of the well-known peaks in and around the Lake Tahoe Basin can give a hiker the feeling of being on top of the world. Same with Twin Peaks, just without the time commitment or exertion of a Tallac or Freel.

For those who live near this South Shore outdoor area, it's a hike that can be done after work when there is enough light.

Twin Peaks is aptly named because it's two peaks in one. Rumor has it those peaks are named after a particular woman who lived in South Lake Tahoe.

What makes it fun is that it's a playground for different users. The easier of two 4-wheel drive routes can even look gnarly depending on the year because of the deep ruts. In the winter it's a great place to snowshoe. In the summer, it's a wonderful hike.

Reaching the first peak, we scrambled up the granite rocks to get the best view. Mount Tallac is to the left, but the sun angle can make it difficult to make out the snow cross. To the right is Lake Tahoe. To Tallac's left was a waterfall in the distance coming out of the mountains — water that isn't usually there. Snow was still visible in the higher elevations.

Behind us is the second peak with the tower on it to warn aircraft. We started on a distinct path toward it, but lost it pretty quickly.

Bushwhacking is the norm on this hike. Not to worry about a trickle of blood here and there.

From the top it's easy to see the planes parked at Lake Tahoe Airport. It is 1.5 miles to the top of the first peak. It's less than one-half mile to the other peak. However, mileage will depend on your route there and back.

Tallac Site: Historical Walk Includes Two Lakes

Scenic: 6
Challenge: 3
Special note: Signage is lacking.
Getting there: From South Lake Tahoe, take Highway 89 north to Camp Richardson. Turn right to park at the Grove restaurant. Begin walking to the left of the restaurant at the beach and into the Tallac Site. If you see signs for Taylor Creek Visitor Center, follow those. Then take the Rainbow Trail. Cross the highway on the other side of the stream profile center. Go up Cathedral Road. A dirt trail juts off from the road to the left. From there, stay to the left to find the dam. (There are no signs.) Keep walking and you'll hit the campground. That leads you to Fallen Leaf Lake Road, which goes to Highway 89. Cross the highway and follow the bike path to Camp Richardson.

Tahoe's past, present and possible future unfold along the shores of Lake Tahoe and Fallen Leaf Lake on an easy 5-mile trek that never gets old.

Meandering through the estates of the Tallac Site on the South Shore, the buildings of yesteryear dot the landscape. If only they could talk. Life in the Lake Tahoe Basin was much different when the Baldwins, Hellers and Popes called this lakefront oasis home.

Now it's a historic site on land owned by the U.S. Forest Service. In the summer it's more populated with tourists and the buildings are in use. The old boathouse is a theater. The grand hall is used for weddings and other functions.

Markers along the way tell the story of how these buildings came to be.

Walking close to the shore, the lake looks cold and uninviting in the winter. Just the opposite is the case in summer.

We came to Taylor Creek Visitors Center and walked through the Rainbow Trail. In winter the dead foliage looks otherworldly, while in the fall it's perfect for leaf peepers. Summer weekends it can be crazy busy, as is the fall when the kokanee salmon make their annual migration to spawn.

The four of us crossed Highway 89 to go up Cathedral Road. We got off the road and headed onto the dirt trail as the road goes to the right.

We crossed the dam at Fallen Leaf Lake. That too is old. Anita Baldwin put up the money for it to be built in 1934.

We came out at the campground, then headed across the highway again back to our vehicles parked at the Grove restaurant.

The scenery is always changing with the lakes, meadow and forest. It's a great trek no matter the time of year, though with snow it would be more challenging.

Lam Watah Trail: Flat Trek To Beach

Scenic: 6
Challenge: 1
Special note: Dogs allowed on the west end of the beach.
Getting there: From South Lake Tahoe, head east on Highway 50. Go past the Stateline casinos. Turn left on Kahle Drive. The parking area is immediately on the right.

History and natural beauty come together in a magical way along the easy Lam Watah Trail.

"This beautiful piece of land has many fascinating connections to the past. For centuries, the Washoe used it as a summer encampment. It has been logged, and grazed by cattle," reads the interpretive sign. "Pony Express riders came through here, and it was home of Tahoe's first airport. Most recently, two full-scale casinos were almost built here."

Improvements to the area by the U.S. Forest Service have made it an even more pleasurable trek. Mini walkways have been installed over the low areas. Signs explain a bit about what is in this meadow. The Forest Service has owned this plot of land on the South Shore since the 1980s.

Rabe Meadow is a place to visit in every season. Like so much of Lake Tahoe, it has something special to share every month.

Burke Creek weaves along the western edge, bringing lushness to some areas.

The main trail is completely flat, creating a meandering jaunt that ends at Nevada Beach, with a short jog through the campground. It's about 3 miles round trip.

The splendor of the beach competes against the meadow for which is most spectacular.

To avoid lots of people, go in the off season when the campground is not full. Fall is a wonderful time to visit.

This is one of those outings where it's about the walk, the beauty, the solitude, as well as the company of the one you're with. It's not about endurance or speed or working up a sweat.

Pony Express Trail: Following Pioneers' Footsteps

Scenic: 4
Challenge: 4
Special note: Not well populated; might want to go with others.
Getting there: From South Lake Tahoe, take Highway 50 west to the top of Echo Summit. Park at Adventure Mountain. The trail is to the right, almost immediately as you turn in.

Casually walking along the Pony Express Trail we wondered how pioneers had the gumption to push on through the Sierra.

Hiking with ample water and modern clothing is a breeze. And we had a map. To have done so with wagons, cumbersome clothing and at times with inadequate supplies on roads that, well, weren't roads, is a bit mindboggling.

These thoughts crossed our minds as the three of us hiked this stretch of land. We did a 7.5-mile out-and-back from Echo Summit to the road that goes to Sierra-at-Tahoe, walking on a trail to the south of Highway 50. It is part of the Pony Express Trail, Pacific Crest Trail and links to the Tahoe Rim Trail.

While it is part of wildly popular trails, it's not well used by the day hiker.

Besides being relatively secluded, what made this hike a bit unique was the changing terrain. Starting out we were treated to a wall of granite that made us pause with its grandeur.

At times we were on a road; other times on single-track dirt. Signs posted for a trail run that was over kept us going in the correct direction. Even without them we would not have gotten lost.

It didn't take long for Lake Audrain to come into view. It looked like quite a descent, which meant an even more strenuous climb out. We opted to forego that side trip and headed forward.

Much of the trail is up and down, with nothing too extreme either way.

Bushes with spikey berries were something new for each of us to see. Ferns filled several sections. This lushness meant there were a couple spots where AJ could get running water.

We were treated to a couple of eagles soaring overhead. Their screeching is what first got our attention.

Once we got to the road at Sierra, we had a bite to eat before turning around.

Hawley Grade Falls: No Crowds

Scenic: 3
Challenge: 5
Special note: Trail can be wet in the early season.
Getting there: From South Lake Tahoe, go west on Highway 50 to Meyers. Pass through town. Turn left on South Upper Truckee Road. Go almost to the end. On the right, there will be a U.S. Forest Service gate. Park near it and start walking.

Express delivery of mail was probably slowed down a bit depending on the time of year as men on horseback crossed the Hawley Grade Falls.

Also called the Upper Truckee Falls, this trek in Meyers used to be part of the Pony Express route. It was used from April-November 1860, after which time the trail was altered to go along Johnson Pass Road.

In spring and early summer usually enough thundering water is descending at a rapid pace that it's best not to cross the falls.

Some years, evidence of the winter's high winds is in abundance with large trees blocking the trail. We scampered over them to reach our destination.

In 2008, a 75-foot section was taken out in a landslide. The U.S. Forest Service stabilized the lower slope.

Going up, the roar of the falls bounces off the towering pines. Soon the cascading icy water comes into view. It's like a series of mini-waterfalls tumbling over granite boulders to form one long fall that eventually reaches the Upper Truckee River.

Manzanita was just beginning to bloom. Closer to the river the distinctive red willow branches were clustered together. Much of the trail was dry, though spots can be muddy in the spring.

We heard something scurry in the brush. Kim's dog, Joe, on a previous hike up Hawley Grade, ended up at the vet's office after tangling with a porcupine.

One of the best things about going in spring is the absence of mountain bikers. They prefer when the water is a trickle or non-existent so they can keep going up to Echo Summit or descend from there into Meyers.

Hawley Grade gets its name from Asa Hawley, a pioneer on the South Shore. This was reportedly the first graded wagon road crossing the Sierra.

Besides being a National Recreation Trail, this route is said to be an area where Snowshoe Thompson saved someone's life.

It's about 1.5 miles to the falls, with an elevation gain of about 900 feet. Sturdy shoes are recommended. It's narrow in spots, but most people will be able to do this hike.

Cascade Falls: Short Hike, Long Falls

Scenic: 3
Challenge: 3
Special note: Go in the morning before the trail gets crowded.
Getting there: From South Lake Tahoe, go north on Highway 89. After the hairpin turns, look for the Bayview Campground on the left. Park there. The trailhead is at the far end of the campground. A sign points left to Cascade Falls and right to Desolation Wilderness.

Songbirds were singing a tune that seemed to say, "Welcome to our little piece of paradise." We smiled as we entered their world.

Soon the roar of Cascade Falls filled our ears. In the distance we could see it cascading into its namesake. A lone fishing boat was on the glass-like water of Cascade Lake.

From this vantage point, Cascade Falls is more impressive than it is when you are right on top of it.

The main fall is 200-feet long. In heavy snow years, the water may be tumbling well into summer. This can result in nearby offshoots of water being visible when walking the trail and up close.

Rated "easy" by the U.S. Forest Service, this trail is extremely popular. If seclusion is what you are looking for, drive on by. If the grandeur of Mother Nature is what's calling you, hike the less than 1 mile to the falls.

Beauty is everywhere. What can be challenging is having a dog on a leash who wants to go faster than you over the rocks and your balance comes into question. It is the up and down of the rocks that can provide some difficulty. Poles are recommended for anyone who likes a bit more stability.

I wouldn't recommend it for little dogs, but that didn't stop others on the trail. There are quite a few granite "stairs" which can be trying for an infirmed dog or people with bad knees. I definitely would not walk it in sandals, but people were. Still, this is a hike most anyone can do.

Approaching along the granite-lined trail, the noise of what sounds like a freight train grows louder. Then the falls come into view. It's one of those moments to remember because pictures can't do this scene justice.

It's as though a spigot is attached to the wall of granite in this corner of Desolation Wilderness. The catch basin is the private Cascade Lake.

At the top of the falls are what looks like several waterways tripping over the smooth granite dotted with trees and bushes. They form one large swath as they go over the side as the waterfall.

Cascade Lake and Lake Tahoe are visible from the top.

Late spring, early summer are the best times to see Cascade Falls because of the gushing water. Just don't be in a rush. People and beauty are apt to slow you down. It's not recommended when there is still snow on the trail.

South Shore/ American River Canyon Snowshoes

"There's just something beautiful about walking on snow that nobody else has walked on."

— *Carol Rifka Brunt*

Roundabout: Not A Green Run Going Uphill

Scenic: 8
Challenge: 7
Special note: Don't go when there are skiers.
Getting there: From South Lake Tahoe, turn onto Ski Run Boulevard. Turn left on Needle Peak Road, right on Wildwood Avenue, left on Saddle Road, right on Keller Road, and right on Sherman Way. The road dead-ends at Sherman. There is a gate there. Start walking.

Solitude. Blue. Calm. Incredible. Inspirational. Awe. These are just a few of the words that came to mind while looking at Lake Tahoe from the top of Gunbarrel at Heavenly Mountain Resort.

It's a limited window when one can snowshoe this route. It must be before the ski season opens or after it ends. It is an impossible snowshoe during the ski season; too many people are on skis on what seems like a narrow path. On snowshoes, it's like being on a road — wide, with plenty of room.

Roundabout lives up to its name. The circuitous route is usually the easy way down the mountain to California Lodge. Going up on snowshoes, ascending about 1,600 feet to an elevation of more than 8,200 feet, cannot be described as easy. The beauty, though, takes one's breath away; or maybe that's due to the climb or the altitude.

While it isn't necessary to have poles, it would be a good idea for anyone with knee or balance issues.

Other than the crunching of the snowshoes against the terrain there was silence. Be sure to pause to hear the stillness and appreciate the beauty that seems to change at every corner. Various views of Lake Tahoe spill forth. Mount Tallac and Pyramid Peak stand out at various times. The casinos, while dominant in some ways, seem so insignificant from this vantage point.

The pinnacle is the top of Gunbarrel and the ski resort's tram. This is one view that never gets old. The whole lake unfolds in a breathtaking view that seems almost surreal.

Instead of going back the same way, it was time to see what it's like to snowshoe The Face. A zigzag approach seemed best so as not to tumble and become a snowball that careens to the bottom. It took some patience and focus because some rocks weren't far beneath the snow.

At times the snow was powdery, making the snowshoes a much-needed tool. Too bad the poles were in the garage. Other spots were crusty, making the trek more of a challenge. Instead of going all the way down this route, just like on skis, it's possible to hook up with Roundabout to make it out on a less steep grade.

To do a round trip on Roundabout and skip The Face is just more than 5 miles.

Becker Peak: Summit Is Worth The Effort

Scenic: 8
Challenge: 6
Special note: A sno-park pass is required from Nov. 1-May 30. They are available online.
Getting there: From South Lake Tahoe, take Highway 50 west over Echo Summit. Turn right on Johnson Pass Road. Parking is to the right.

Crevasses and the refraction of light had Echo Lake looking like it mirrored a sky filled with puffy cumulus clouds. It was as though a pale blue marker had been used to draw circles on the white sheet of ice.

From our vantage point atop Becker Peak and then walking along the ridge, Echo Lake was mesmerizing. Nine of us spent a morning snowshoeing to the top of Becker Peak — elevation 8,391 feet.

Snowshoeing in drought years requires seeking out higher elevations because it's only dirt at lake level. This is one route that should be good no matter what it looks like at lake level in the winter. While some of us were in shorts and others in short sleeves on this warm spring day, the snowshoes were definitely needed. Snow even covered the road leading to Echo Lake.

A late morning start was ideal so the snow had some give to it. Almost everyone used poles, which was good on the steeper sections for the ascent and decline. The worst part, at least in terms of exertion, is turning off the road and heading straight up to the ridge. We made the left directly across from the Berkeley Camp and by a few no parking signs.

SOUTH SHORE/AMERICAN RIVER CANYON/SNOWSHOES

Some in the group advised that it's better to start a little farther up the road during hiking season to avoid what is bushy terrain without snow.

If the route up does not take your breath away, the views on top of the ridge are bound to. Flagpole, Angora Peak, Dicks Peak, the back of Mount Tallac, Jakes Peak, the Angora burn area and Lake Tahoe all spill forth in an array of winter beauty. While it would be possible to call it a day at this point in terms of scenic beauty, the views only get better.

Even though Craig, a snowshoer in our party, was correct to say the hard part was over, there was still some climbing to do. I was glad to be with people who had done this trek before. Even though other snowshoers had laid down a trail before us, their route was a bit sketchy at times. Some said there was no way to get lost, but I also believe there is a first for everything.

Not too much farther and we saw the slopes of Sierra-at-Tahoe on our left and a frozen Echo Lake to our right. We got to what could be another stopping point where there was an incredible expansive view of Echo Lake. We paused long enough for photos before making the final ascent to Becker Peak.

The peak itself is a pile of large rocks. Off came the snowshoes so we could scramble to the top. Even AJ the dog was able to make it up to the top. We sat there a bit, having a bite to eat, taking in the views and putting layers back on to ward off the nippy wind. It was 360 degrees of pure Sierra serenity.

Skiers were along the edge of Echo Lake. Talking Mountain, from this vantage point, looks like it would be easy to reach. We climbed about 1,000 feet to get to this point. It's about 4.5 miles round trip. We chose a lower route back that provided more views of Echo Lake and Lake Tahoe.

Emerald Bay: Without Vehicle Traffic

Scenic: 8
Challenge: 3
Special note: This snowshoe trek is not available every winter. Caltrans will have road closure information.
Getting there: From South Lake Tahoe, go north on Highway 89. There will be a gate across the highway; park where you can.

Cascade Lake looked like it needed a Zamboni machine to clear off the snow to make it a perfect skating rink. Emerald Bay was eerily black, as though perhaps some creature of the lake lurked below. Tahoe Tessie?

It was one of those rare winter opportunities when Highway 89 was closed to vehicles and open to foot traffic. Parking at the gate near the entrance to Eagle Point Campground, we strapped on snowshoes to make the 1.1-mile trek to appropriately named Inspiration Point.

Fortunately, someone beat us there so we didn't have to break trail. Only one path heads up the road — wide enough for snowshoes, but a definite single file approach. Meandering up the hairpin turns, going slower than the 10 mph limit, we came to one of the most scenic areas in the Lake Tahoe Basin. The private Cascade Lake is to our left, Emerald Bay on our right, and behind us Lake Tahoe. Cascade looked frozen — as if a hockey game or figure skating competition should be under way.

As the M.S. Dixie II paddle-wheeler churned into Emerald Bay, the normal blue water looked foreboding. Ice lingered on the edge near Vikingsholm castle, signaling just how cold the water was. Fannette

Island was dusted in snow from a recent storm, making the teahouse look almost like a gingerbread house sprinkled with powder sugar.

The snow was light, the air cool. Traipsing up we were warmed by the sun, but as soon as we paused at the lookout area, we were chilled in the shade. We didn't linger long, having many times before read the informative interpretive signs explaining what we were looking at and how glaciers formed these bodies of water. They are worth reading for first-timers or to get a refresher about the area's history.

Heading back, it was as though we were surrounded by water now that Lake Tahoe was in front of us. It was truly magical, especially because this isn't something one can do every day or even every winter. Highway 89 closes throughout the winter because of avalanche conditions and heavy snowfall, so it's hit or miss when this snowshoe route is an option.

Fallen Leaf Lake: A Wintertime Wonder

Scenic: 7
Challenge: 3
Special note: A sno-park permit is required. The permits may be bought online.
Getting there: From South Lake Tahoe, head north on Highway 89. Go through Camp Richardson. Pass the turn for Fallen Leaf Lake. Cathedral Road is on the left.

Strapping on our snowshoes in the Cathedral Road parking lot off Highway 89 we began our journey into the wild. At least it seemed that way as the quiet enveloped us.

The snow-covered road was wide enough to stride along in pairs and not be knocked over by one of our four-legged friends. At times the trail narrowed from the thick conifers, then suddenly it was as though there was a meadow of snow.

Not far in we veered to the left to take the trail instead of staying on the road even though no motor vehicles can drive on it with snow on the ground. It became single track. One by one we sauntered forward. At times water crossed our path, necessitating a bit of improvising. This can happen in the early and late seasons depending on the snowfall accumulations and the subsequent melt.

Taylor Creek was flowing toward Lake Tahoe at what looked like capacity and it wasn't even spring yet.

Onward we went, heading to Fallen Leaf Lake to the left instead of going right which would have us loop back to the parking lot. Up and over the dam with snowshoes on takes a bit of dexterity and concentration.

Contrails lined the blue sky, crossing through the wispy clouds to create a one-of-a-kind canvas. The still water reflected the mountains of Desolation Wilderness until the canines sent ripples across the alpine lake.

Break time meant peeling off clothes as the sun beat down on us. Most of the dogs ventured into Fallen Leaf Lake to retrieve sticks, unfazed by the ice floating nearby.

Back we went, though not exactly as we had come. We ended up making a loop to our left, through what during late summer is one of the most incredible patches of lupine. On this day it was the stark white bark of the aspen grove that captured our attention.

From the parking lot to the dam is about 1 mile. It's possible to spend all day in this area exploring.

Tallac Site: Window To The South Shore's Past

Scenic: 7
Challenge: 2
Special note: Good for all ages.
Getting there: From South Lake Tahoe, go north on Highway 89 toward Emerald Bay. At Camp Richardson, turn right at the lodge. Drive down to the parking lot at the Grove restaurant. Tallac Site is to the left.

Apparently for rich San Franciscans, Lake Tahoe's winters were too harsh. Instead of embracing the elements and the beauty, they boarded up their homes, packed their belongings and went to the flat land for most of the year. Of course, those who summered on the shores of Lake Tahoe in the first half of the 20th century didn't have all the modern conveniences we have today.

Had those with last names like Pope, Baldwin and Heller decided to reside year-round at what is now known as the Tallac Historic Site, it's possible the winter experience would be much different. Maybe it would still be privately owned and off-limits to the rest of us.

Today, it is so incredibly tranquil. Few people venture to this part of the South Shore in winter. It's almost like a ghost town. Sure, the buildings there are closed up just like when the area was privately owned. But there is still plenty to see. The U.S. Forest Service has done a great job putting up signs telling about the history of this site.

Nineteen buildings are dispersed on what were three estates. (Most are open in the summer.) The 74 acres are listed on the National Register of Historic Places. Restoration work continues on the buildings and grounds.

Imagine what it would have been like a century ago to live here. Imagine the summers back then compared to today. Same lake, same trees, same beach — but a different time makes for a different world. This trek is a bit present day, a bit yesteryear.

It's possible to end up at Baldwin Beach. Going along the beach back to the parking lot is an option instead of returning through the Tallac Site. Routes make it so it can be a loop or an out-and-back. This also means the mileage can vary. Plan on it being close to 3 miles round trip. This trek is good on snowshoes, cross country skis and snow boots.

Baldwin Beach: A Shoreline Jaunt

Scenic: 7
Challenge: 2
Special note: Pay attention to the no parking signs along the highway to avoid being towed.
Getting there: From South Lake Tahoe, go north on Highway 89. Park at the gate for Baldwin Beach where it says "Recreation Area Closed for the Season." If you reach Cascade Properties, you went too far.

The few feet of sand next to the lake may have one thinking a towel and book would be good things to bring next time. This happens on winter days that feel more like spring. The snow had softened enough by late morning to have a little give and made walking pleasurable. Lake Tahoe was like glass, beckoning anyone foolish enough to come play with her. But we knew better. She is no friend this time of year — this icy bowl of water.

Outdoor enthusiasts had laid several tracks. An etiquette reminder: if possible, don't walk in the tracks of cross country skiers. Even though dogs are not allowed, people have left behind evidence their pets were there.

Meandering down what looks like a forested tunnel due to thick conifers on either side had altered my state of mind. I'm lost in this wonderland. Inhaling, exhaling. Oh, that mountain air. Less than a mile in, the terrain opened, and Lake Tahoe's deep blue waters were just steps away. We headed north along the beach. Mount Tallac was to our left covered with snow.

No one was in sight, yet the tracks proved plenty of people had beaten us to this little slice of Tahoe splendor. We went as far as we could. A creek prevented us from crossing. Although the water level was low, there would be no way not to get our feet wet. No matter the outside temperature, wet feet can lead to frostbite. At times this inlet can be crossed on the ice. However, crossing any ice in Tahoe is tricky because of the freeze-thaw factor. It's not always as solid as one might think it is. When the area is crossable, it becomes a bit of an architectural tour with all the shoreline homes.

We turned around and headed toward Taylor Creek. A large predator bird was circling in the distance — perhaps a hawk of some sort. It's one of those incredibly easy outings, whether on snowshoes or cross country skis, because it's all flat. No chance of getting lost with the lake on one side. It is one of the most scenic places to visit – even more so in the winter than summer.

Maggie's Peak: Views All Along The Way

Scenic: 6
Challenge: 7
Special note: Go early because parking can be an issue.
Getting there: From South Lake Tahoe, go north on Highway 89. Park at the Bayview Campground on the left. This is before the parking lot for Vikingsholm. Walk through the campground. There will be a sign indicating left for Cascade Falls, right for Desolation Wilderness. Go right.

Maggie's cleavage took our breath away.

That's what we called the saddle of Maggie's Peak because, well, these two peaks in Desolation Wilderness are named for a woman who was well endowed. That strip of land in between the peaks has some outstanding views.

Desolation Wilderness appears to go on forever. So expansive it seems a bit foreboding, even though we were immersed in it for nearly the entire snowshoe. No wonder Eagle Lake is chilly in the summer; it's often frozen in the winter. On this particular day Emerald Bay could have been renamed Sapphire Bay because of the rich, deep blue hue that spilled forth.

Snowshoeing to Granite Lake was pretty, while the final push to the saddle of Maggie's Peak was spectacular. Granite Lake was our original destination. Getting there was more of a vertical ascent than a leisurely switchback. This was not a trek on which to set speed records, so Donna, Rosemary, Sue and I — and dogs AJ and Cody — stopped several times along the way.

The path was well worn with plenty of snowshoers having been there before us. It's single track. At times all we could hear was the crunching of the snow beneath the claws strapped to our boots.

Large boulders near Granite Lake and protruding from the ice provided a lunch spot. Plenty of tracks across the frozen mass proved the ice was thick. Not a cloud could be seen. It was one of those idyllic Tahoe blue skies. One of Maggie's Peaks rose from the far end of the lake.

Donna and Sue perused the map, figuring out the cleavage wasn't that much farther, so we carried on. The trailhead is at 6,890 feet. Granite Lake is at 7,700 feet and the saddle is at 8,330 feet. It's about 1½ miles to the lake and another eight-tenths of a mile to the saddle. While there had been wonderful views along the way, the best were definitely at the saddle.

Van Sickle Park: The Country's Only Bi-State Park

Scenic: 6
Challenge: 5
Special note: Free parking is difficult to find. Casino valet may be an option.
Getting there: From the South Shore, turn on Heavenly Village Way. This dead ends at the park. Paid parking is available at a garage on Bellamy Court, which is off Heavenly Village Way.

Everything changes with a little snow. Some things even get better, like the views from Van Sickle Bi-State Park.

While we were familiar with the trail, we were thankful others had gone before us to ensure we were going in the correct direction. This 725-acre park on the South Shore provides stunning views of Lake Tahoe by snowshoeing just a short distance. The scenic outlook is a mere 0.4 miles from the trailhead.

One problem in winter is the required walking to get to the trailhead. The California Tahoe Conservancy and Nevada Division of State Lands, which own and operate the park, shut the entrance gate from Nov. 1-April 30. With nearby casinos eliminating free parking, parking can be a bit of a conundrum.

There is a distinct trail almost directly across from Harrah's casino's back parking lot. Warning: it can be a bit precarious to cross the street without a crosswalk.

We sauntered up a little hill and then went left on South Tahoe Public Utility District's road before we took a left onto the park's road. A trail sign clearly indicates where the path really begins. It's also possible to start at the gate to the park at the intersection of Montreal Road and Heavenly Village Parkway.

With part of the actual path a bit icy, it was great to have the claws of snowshoes to dig into the terrain. However, patches of dirt had to be walked on, too. Conditions will depend on the time of year and the amount of snow that winter.

Climbing to the vista is well worth the views of Lake Tahoe and the mountain peaks. The Stateline casinos, Rabe Meadow and Round Hill stand out as well.

Tracks from other snowshoers, hikers and cross country skiers were evident. Even super wide bike tires had left their mark in the snow. It's a great place for dogs, too.

Signs tell people about the terrain as well as where to go. The Gondola Fire of 2002 is talked about because many of the charred trees remain in the park. The story of sugar pine plantings is also posted.

We took the upper turnoff for the Cal/Neva Loop. It heads toward California, with a spur going to the Saddle Road neighborhood. It was quiet, even secluded. At one point the pines gave us a sense of being enclosed in some far-off winter wonderland. The snow was softer, powder-like. Fewer people had been there. Lake Tahoe was glassy and inviting, if only it weren't so darn cold.

Starting after noon meant the temps were warmer and the afternoon light provided colors and contrasts different than those cast by Mother Nature in the morning. Soon we were reminded how close to civilization we were as the Heavenly Mountain Resort gondola whirred above us.

We took the Barn Trail, knowing it would lead us to the main park road that would drop us off near the park's entrance. With the abundance of trails, mileage is going to vary. Check out this link to get a map with distances:
http://parks.nv.gov/forms/VanSickle_Bi_State_Park_Map.pdf.

Angora Ridge:
Views In Multiple Directions

Scenic: 6
Challenge: 5
Special note: Parking is a problem.
Getting there: From South Lake Tahoe, at the Y go straight on Lake Tahoe Boulevard toward South Tahoe High School or the Angora burn area. Turn right on Tahoe Mountain Road. Go right at the T intersection. Go left at the next T. The road curves a bit. Go slow. Parking in front of the gate at the start of the trail is the best bet to avoid being towed.

The trek to Angora Ridge, like most routes going uphill, is all about the conditions. When it's slick, it's about having good claws to grab the hard pack snow. Breaking trail is a workout. It's a climb, no doubt about that. But the views — oh, they're worth it.

The 1.8 miles can feel a bit longer than that, which could be because the ridge is a thousand feet higher than lake level. It was five of us and a dog on this day, heading to the lookout at an elevation of 7,256 feet. The start was deceiving because of how flat it was — meadow-like, really. With this being a road, it is wide enough to walk side by side.

The others were in front of us chattering away; their loss because mom and I were sure an eagle, with its distinctive wingspan and white markings, flew overhead. Bald eagles are common in this part of Tahoe.

Up we went in almost a straight path. No switchbacks to contend with. Mount Tallac was visible to our right through the looming conifers. Gradually some charred trees come into sight to our left, remnants of the 2007 Angora Fire that burned about 3,100 acres, mostly U.S. Forest Service land. It was this federal property that we were on. From the ridge, the Angora burn area was unmistakable. New houses prove the resilience of the 254 homeowners who lost their homes. Many of the matchstick-like trees still stand.

The old fire lookout remains on top of Angora Ridge. A Forest Service forester built it in 1924. It was converted into a residence for Civilian Conservation Corps members, who in 1935 built a larger lookout nearby. No longer is this an active fire lookout. However, the buildings are eligible for inclusion on the National Register of Historic Places.

Looking north is Fallen Leaf Lake, with the base of Mount Tallac seeming to touch the far shore.

Up another mile is the parking lot for Angora Lakes Resort, with its two lakes. During the summer, the eight cabins are available for rent. Dogs must be leashed and are not allowed in the lakes. Opened in the 1920s, the resort is so popular that it's usually booked a year in advance.

This trek is doable for experienced cross country skiers. It is more difficult on skis than snowshoes because of the climb and descent.

Echo Lake Ridge: Full Of Beauty

Scenic: 6
Challenge: 4
Special note: A sno-park pass is required from Nov. 1-May 30. They are available online.
Getting there: From South Lake Tahoe, go west on Highway 50 to the top of Echo Summit. Turn right on Johnson Pass Road. Follow the road to the sno-park area. Cross the road and begin the trek on the road to Echo Lake.

A short jaunt up to the ridge above Echo Lake was a much-needed reminder of just how gorgeous this area is. Sometimes it's easy to take the beauty of the greater Lake Tahoe area for granted when one is immersed in daily life.

Stripped down to short sleeves — two of the five on the outing were in shorts — it was a glorious spring day. Not a cloud was in the sky. A cool breeze greeted us as we hiked farther on the ridge.

It's amazing how in less than 1½ miles we had a spectacular view of what seemed like the entire Tahoe basin. Mostly, though, it was the South Shore that spilled forth. At that elevation it was a good reminder of how this really is a forest and not a concrete jungle.

On this particular day the road to Echo Lake was wide, matted down and easy to walk without snowshoes. Two in our group had been there just a couple weeks before when it was a different world because of the fresh snow. Then the snow was a couple feet deep, making it much more of a workout. That's the thing about playing in the snow; conditions will vary.

We passed by the frozen lake, crossed the dam and headed up to get to the point where we'd get that view. Others, though, had stopped to play on the frozen Lower Echo Lake — cross country skiing and skate skiing. Once across the dam we all had our snowshoes on.

We opted to head toward Flagpole Peak (elevation 8,363 feet). At one point we turned around to look down on some of the devices used for avalanche control above Highway 50.

It's the 360-degree views that make this such a great jaunt. It's relatively easy, and at just less than 3½ miles round trip, it should be done every year. Besides seeing Lake Tahoe in the distance, there are iconic peaks like Freel and Becker scratching the sky.

Twin Peaks:
Short Scamper, Big Views

Scenic: 6
Challenge: 4
Special note: Good for most ages.
Getting there: From the Y in South Lake Tahoe, continue on Lake Tahoe Boulevard. Turn left on Sawmill Road. Park immediately in the lot to the left.

Easy, fun, scenic. Scampering up Twin Peaks on snowshoes encompasses all of these elements.

It's one of those jaunts that is great on a day when you want a little exercise outdoors, but don't have a ton of time. Of course, snow conditions always play a role in how long an excursion will take. It's also one of those sojourns where, if it's a warm day, it's worth lingering a bit. The views are some of the best for so little effort. The top provides an ideal lunch spot and place to sit with a book, or to just meditate a while, remembering why Lake Tahoe is so special.

Beneath us the snow was firm. It was nice to have the claws on the shoes so we didn't slip. Although the route is not extremely steep, it is definitely uphill without any plateaus to change the pitch. This is a fun 4-wheel drive road in the summer. Being a road, it's wide enough to walk side by side.

Fully exposed, we welcomed the sun on this chilly late January afternoon. Turning around, the views of the Sierra unfolded. The ridges looked uninviting in some ways. Maybe that was because I know how much more work they are to climb compared to this little hill.

In the summer it's easy to hit both peaks — it's called Twin Peaks, after all. On the other side is the tower with the warning light for aircraft. From there is a view to Lake Tahoe Airport, Lake Tahoe Golf Course and Meyers. It takes a bit of bushwhacking through the manzanita in summer. That prospect sounded horrible on snowshoes. Instead, we sauntered up by the massive granite boulders to take in views of Lake Tahoe to our right. Angora Ridge, with her barren trees from the 2007 fire by the same name, was stark against the brilliant white snow. Mount Tallac hovered beyond.

This is 3 miles round trip.

Emerald Bay Campground: Silence, Beauty, Emptiness

Scenic: 6
Challenge: 3
Special note: Without snow, there is ample parking off the road.
Getting there: From South Lake Tahoe, take Highway 89 north. Once you go through all the hairpin turns and are about to reach the stretch where Cascade Lake is on the left and Emerald Bay is on the right, the campground is on the right.

While it would have been nice to be able to start a fire at the campsite to warm up a bit, it was even better having the entire campground to ourselves.

As we descended to the shore of Emerald Bay, we walked through a blizzard. Not everyone realized the bay was to our left as we snowshoed down; the visibility was that poor. Fresh snow was gradually accumulating on the already snow-laden picnic tables in Eagle Point Campground.

Trekking through this 100-spot campground on snowshoes is ideal. Seldom is anyone else there. The solitude and tranquility are abundant. It's the scenery that will give you pause and reason to take a camera. Pines and cedar loom tall. Only the crunching of snowshoes can be heard.

Early on there was an opportunity to hook up with the Rubicon Trail. Instead we went to the right, the opposite direction. Mostly we followed the snow-covered road. At one point we meandered off to get a view of the water below. When we reached the bottom-most campsite, we broke trail to reach the bay. There, the water lapped against the rocks. Icicles had formed on some of the vegetation. On the far side of Lake Tahoe, blue sky peaked out. A couple boats braved the winter weather.

Looking around, it was easy to understand why in 1969 Emerald Bay was designated a National Natural Landmark. This campground is part of the larger Emerald Bay State Park, which includes the whole bay and Vikingsholm. The state acquired the land in 1953 from Placerville lumberman Harvey West for half the amount of its appraisal.

Mileage is going to be dependent on how much one meanders around the camping area and along the shore. It's about 1 mile straight down on the road.

High Meadow: Straight Up, Straight Down

Scenic: 5
Challenge: 6
Special note: Note your surroundings because signage is not great.
Getting there: From South Lake Tahoe, turn onto Al Tahoe Boulevard. Turn right on Pioneer Trail. Turn left on Remington Trail. (Sierra House Elementary School is on the corner.) Follow signs to the end and park. On the trail, veer up and to the right.

I had to catch my breath at one point as I felt the pull in my legs and lungs at the same time. "That's why it's called High Meadow," Rosemary said.

Although there was dirt on the route most exposed to the sun, it still seemed easier to hike with snowshoes than just boots. As we kept climbing, the snow got better for this winter activity. Large conifers loomed overhead, casting shadows on this gloriously sunny day. While the temperature was chilly to begin with, the exertion had us losing layers.

Different spurs could have you exploring the High Meadow trail system for days. Star Lake is about six miles one-way. High Meadow is about one mile below the lake. It's possible to make this a long or short snowshoe depending on when you turn around.

In summer 2010, the U.S. Forest Service turned the meadow into a construction zone in order to restore Cold Creek. The evidence is not visible to the untrained eye. What's left is a healthier environment.

On our trek we made it to an earlier manmade disturbance — power lines. Power Line Trail gets its name from all those overhead wires that run through the forest. A vista of sorts beckoned us before we reached our end point. The knoll provided panoramic views in all directions. Lake Tahoe almost looked small below the forest. The clearing we used as a turnaround point provided spectacular views looking west to Mount Tallac, Pyramid Peak and other ridgetops in Desolation Wilderness.

Although signs are clearly posted that snowmobiles are not allowed where we were, the visible tracks prove the sleds had been out. Those tracks always make snowshoeing and cross country skiing easier. With the trail wide enough for a vehicle in places, it allowed us to walk at least two across. This made it easier to hear each other over the crunching of the snow.

Grass Lake: An Easy Escape Atop Luther Pass

Scenic: 5
Challenge: 3
Special note: Make a mental note of where you parked.
Getting there: From South Lake Tahoe, go west on Highway 50. In Meyers, go left onto Highway 89. At the crest of Luther Pass, Grass Lake is on the right. There are several pullouts for parking.

Flat, scenic and free equals perfect snowshoe conditions. Grass Lake is serene much of the winter. Some days the powder is like sugar, so easy to walk through. Others had been there before us so we didn't have to break trail if we didn't want to.

Waterhouse Peak (9,497 feet) is the highest, nearest landmark. And while that may sound like it is towering, Luther Pass, where Grass Lake is, is at 7,740 feet.

When there isn't much snow at lake level, this is an ideal place to snowshoe or cross country ski. Plenty of dogs are often out getting exercise, too. When snow isn't on the ground this is a marshy area. It's not a true lake.

Even though Highway 89 is so close, its activity is only noticeable if you want it to be. That may sound odd, but I'm a firm believer people have the capability to tune out most distractions. The din of traffic is one of them.

Ironically, the three of us welcomed that traffic when we were done. We had committed one of the bigger mistakes while playing in the woods. No one paid attention to our starting point. That meant when we got back to the road we didn't know which way to go.

Renee and I were on the road while Rosemary stayed on the snow, almost parallel to us. We got around a bend and as far as the eye could see were no parked vehicles, just another curve. We thought we should turn around and head toward Hope Valley.

Then the three of us were on the road. It was time to hitchhike. After Rosemary got in a vehicle with a couple, their son and their granddaughter (of course we didn't know that's who they were at that time, or that they were super helpful), I asked Renee if she had gotten the license plate number or knew the make of the vehicle. Neither of us had that information. We knew Rosemary had been correct, that we should have kept going toward Meyers, after the Good Samaritans stopped to tell us they were going to look for our vehicle in the other direction. It wasn't long before Rosemary came driving up in her SUV.

I share this story because combined, the three of us had lived on the South Shore for decades. We're experienced at outdoor play in all seasons. We're normally smart women. For some reason we weren't that day. It was a good reminder that communication is necessary, that it's essential to look in all directions when starting off, and to have a focal point to know what to look for when returning. We were never going to be in danger based on where we were that day, but that might not always be the case. We were lucky. This was an experience we could laugh about as we shook our heads in disbelief.

Lake Tahoe Golf Course: Above Par Fun

Scenic: 5
Challenge: 2
Special note: Sometimes the restaurant/bar is open in the winter.
Getting there: From South Lake Tahoe, go west on Highway 50. The golf course is on the right before hitting the heart of Meyers.

Golf courses offer some of most wonderful snowshoeing opportunities. They are flat, scenic and go on for miles. While golfers might think the trees are close together, winter recreationists find these plots of land to be wide open.

Such is the case with Lake Tahoe Golf Course. This is an 18-hole course for much of the year. In winter a snowmobile concessionaire usually operates there. To the right of the clubhouse is the route to get away from the motorized fun. We started to the left of hole 10.

The noise from the motorized sleds dissipated quickly. The exhaust, though, was noticeable as we returned. It was clearly stinking up the fresh mountain air.

One of the nice things about this trek was that it didn't take long to reach a serene landscape. Plenty of people had been there before us. Snowshoe and cross country ski tracks crisscrossed each other. Some of the ski tracks were so worn it was as if they had been professionally laid.

The snow was perfect this particular day so breaking trail was no big deal, and in many ways was more fun. The give to the snow made it relatively easy to push through and a bit more of a workout than going where others had already gone.

A few bridges across the Upper Truckee River and Angora Creek have barriers to keep snowmobilers out. It means either having to gingerly step over them or taking off your equipment.

Many of the South Shore's more recognizable peaks made themselves known as we went farther: Freel, Jobs, Mount Tallac, and Twin Peaks next door.

The golf course sits on state land, namely Lake Valley State Recreation Area. It abuts Washoe Meadows State Park. There are several access points to both. The golf course provides the most parking, especially on days when parking on a street could be problematic because of snow removal.

Distance is all dependent on how far one goes.

West Shore Hikes

"I like being near the top of a mountain.
One can't get lost here."
— *Wislawa Szymborska*

Eagle Rock:
Big Views With Little Effort

Scenic: 8
Challenge: 3
Special note: Signage for starting point is lacking.
Getting there: From South Lake Tahoe, take Highway 89 north. The trail is between Chamber's Landing and Sunnyside, on the left. There is parking on the left side, but there is no visible trailhead sign that can be seen while driving.

Eagle Rock has to be the easiest hike in Lake Tahoe to get some of the most stunning views. It's like having an eagle's-eye view of the basin.

Eagle Rock has always been popular among those who knew about it. It has gotten even more attention because a designated trail was completed in 2013. It used to require scrambling up the rocky backside to get to the top.

When we scampered up there the dirt trail was narrow, with a gradual climb. It's only 1,800-feet long.

Signs at the trailhead say this is a moderate 1-mile hike. I would say for those who are used to hiking in Tahoe it's an easy hike. The only "difficult" part is a bit of rock scrambling at the top. This might be where poles would come in handy for anyone with balance or knee issues.

It's 250 feet of volcanic rock at the top. This, in itself, makes it such a change from the usual granite that dominates the Lake Tahoe Basin.

Like so many places in the basin, this used to be a special spot for Native Americans. However, white people knew about Eagle Rock in the 1880s. At one time there was a gazebo at the top. With how exposed the area is, it's easy to see how it could be a hot vista in the summer.

There is a California State Lands Commission marker at the top that is dated 1979.

The California Tahoe Conservancy in 1987 acquired the 54.5-acre property that includes Eagle Rock for $450,000. In 2012, the Conservancy completed a more than $4 million restoration project in the Blackwood Creek Watershed. This area contributed more sediment to Lake Tahoe than any other watershed in the basin – more than 1,900 tons a year. This is where Blackwood Creek spills into Lake Tahoe.

The Eagle Rock Trail is in the watershed. Part of it was constructed in 2011, with the second and final phase finished in 2013.

The sweeping views make it a must-do hike. It takes about 15 minutes to get to the top. Rubicon Point and Mount Tallac dominate the southern view. Immediately to the south are Homewood Mountain Resort's ski runs. Heavenly Mountain Resort's upper trails are distinctly outlined. To the rear is Rubicon Peak. Private piers dot the landscape to the north.

Ellis Peak:
Above Average Scenery

Scenic: 7
Challenge: 7
Special note: Take mosquito repellant.
Getting there: From South Lake Tahoe, take Highway 89 north. Beyond Homewood and before Sunnyside in Tahoe City will be a sign for Kaspian Campground. Turn left. The road goes for about 7 miles. (Veer to the left and don't go straight on the dirt road.) At the end of the hill, the pavement turns to dirt. The trail is to the left. Park on the side of the road.

If you survive the first half hour, the rest of the hike will feel like an average walk in the woods. However, there is nothing average about the views.

This is what the six of us discovered as we climbed the 8,740-foot Ellis Peak. The total elevation gain is 1,465 feet. A significant amount of it comes right at the start. The reward is so worth it.

It's like walking into a watercolor painting. A sea of colorful wildflowers covered the expansive meadow, including mule's ear, Western blue flax, Indian paintbrush, thistle, and other flora no one knew the name of filling the plateau.

To our right was Loon Lake with its island and other points in the Crystal Basin, along with views of Granite Chief Wilderness Area. Desolation Wilderness is in the other direction.

We marveled at the ruggedness and rather daunting drop-offs. Even from this spot it's a bit like being on top of the world.

It only got better.

The trail is well maintained. Much of it is soft dirt. Shade kept us cool.

In one section trees were covered in moss on all sides so if we were lost, there would be no knowing which direction was north.

Crossing the road that is open to four-wheelers was no big deal. We never saw nor heard any motorized vehicles.

At times Lake Tahoe came into view. Along the trail is seemed so far away.

We scampered up a rock formation we thought was the top of Ellis Peak. We ate lunch, took pictures and congratulated ourselves. Then we looked to our left and saw people on another peak. Oops. Down we went to the real Ellis Peak.

It wasn't that much farther, but pride insisted if we had gotten that far, we were going to make it to our true destination.

In one direction is Lake Tahoe. We are so high that we see behind the basin; the Pine Nut range is in the far distance.

At the base of Ellis is the lake by the same name. From this perch it looked dark and dank, like some backwoods Mississippi swamp.

A structure in the foreground looking toward Lake Tahoe is the top of one of Homewood Mountain Resort's chairlifts. If it were operating, it looks like it would take off substantial time in terms of hiking Ellis Peak.

To avoid the false summit, stay to the right as you near what looks like the peak. We missed the cairns on the way up, but they were clearly there on the way back. The true summit cannot be seen at this point.

The route is about 6.5 miles round trip.

Homewood: Tahoe Unfolds Below

Scenic: 7
Challenge: 7
Special note: Homewood Mountain Resort sometimes has trail maps online or at the guest services office at the North Lodge.
Getting there: From South Lake Tahoe, go north on Highway 89. The ski resort is on the left in Homewood. Plenty of parking. Trails start from the north and south lodges. The north is the main area. The south is at the end of Tahoe Ski Bowl Way, which is off Highway 89. We parked at the main parking lot, walked through the neighborhood and started on the Homeward Connector Trail.

Straight up. That's one way to define what a black diamond hiking trail is.

Ski resort hiking is nothing like being in the forest or in a state or national park. The routes don't follow the contour of the mountain. Switchbacks are unheard of. Instead, many of the trails are straight up or straight down; the better for when snow covers the dirt and skiers are making tracks.

We didn't let the uphill climb deter us even though we whined a bit. AJ, with her four legs, didn't seem to mind the vertical ascent as she ran in front of us.

The owners of Homewood Mountain Resort opened the trails to hiking in 2013. While the legend on the map rates the trails at "less difficult," "more difficult," and "most difficult," the majority fall into the latter. One trail we came down was a double black diamond because of the steepness.

It doesn't take long for a view of Lake Tahoe to appear. That's the thing about Homewood — the views of the lake are the best of any ski resort. You are so close. When skiing the face, it's like you're going to land in the water.

And while the hiking is free, various signs caution people that the trails are not patrolled. Trail markers are signs attached to a round of wood. This just adds to the funkiness.

Before we reached the top of the Quail lift with its vast views, we had taken the Sunnyside Loop that took us to Quail Lake. Barely a ripple could be seen. The calmness and warm surface temperature lured us to take a dip.

AJ had beaten us to the water. She took a shortcut through the thicket.

Lily pads covered much of the lake. Dragonflies and minnows were the only wildlife we saw.

Above us was a wall of ski runs: Main Cirque, 55 Chutes, Wally's Folly and The Shoulder. While patches of color dotted the mountain, winter seemed so far away as we basked in the sun. Snowmaking machines at various locations reminded us where we were.

A log was perfectly placed by the lake as a great spot to have a bite to eat. We essentially had the mountain to ourselves. At times Rubicon Peak stands out above all others. Most of the trails are soft dirt, wood chips or loose rocks.

We hooked up with the Homeward Bound Trail that leads to Cedar Ridge Trail. Finally, we were walking on level ground, not uphill. This is where those picture postcard views of Lake Tahoe happen. It's like you can see the entire lake — all shores. To the north were boats at Sunnyside, to the south we could see the hut on the pier at Chambers Landing, while across the lake is the East Shore.

To reach the base we eased down the double black diamond Ore Car Trail. This is when those with bad knees would welcome poles to finish the approximately 5-mile hike.

Tahoe-Yosemite Trail: A Fraction Of The Trail

Scenic: 6
Challenge: 6
Special note: Best to do later in the summer or early fall.
Getting there: From South Lake Tahoe, take Highway 89 north to Meeks Bay. Just past the fire station on the right, there is parking on the left in the dirt. A small paved lot exists where the actual trailhead starts. Be sure to fill out the free Desolation Wilderness permit.

Only 172 more miles and we would have been in Tuolumne Meadows. It's a good thing we never intended to go to Yosemite National Park.

Plenty of people with the proper equipment were headed out of the wilderness with full packs. All ages, and many families had clearly spent at least one night under the stars.

Instead, we spent the afternoon visiting the first five lakes out of Meeks Bay along the 180-mile Tahoe-Yosemite Trail. The entire trek ranges in elevation from 5,200 feet to 10,000 feet. Between the end points it crosses the Eldorado and Stanislaus national forests.

What sets this apart from so many routes in Desolation Wilderness are the abundance of ferns and other lush vegetation. Many West Shore routes are best accessed later in the season because the snow lasts longer there.

A few wildflowers may still be in bloom in August. It's the array of flora that is captivating.

With a good portion of the trail not being riddled with roots or rocks, it allows hikers to take in the beauty without worrying about tripping and falling.

I imagine the meadow is hiding a bevy of animal life that has taken cover with the plodding footsteps of humans.

Don't be fooled by how the trail starts. It's wide enough for a vehicle, flat and lulls one into believing this is an easy hike. Not far up, the trail juts to the right and becomes single-track. Then the hiking really begins. It's not hard, it's just not flat and wide.

Still, the mix of plant life in this section is mesmerizing. We are thankful for the tree canopy. Without it we would have created puddles of sweat.

Much of the time Meeks Creek can be heard rumbling nearby as it tumbles over rocks in its path. On occasion, it even comes into sight. It eventually flows into Lake Tahoe at Meeks Bay.

First stop is Lake Genevieve. The tranquil water beckoned. If you only have time for a short hike, this is a perfect spot to stop, have a bite to eat, even wade into the alpine waters.

Next up is Crag Lake. The rock island with a tree growing out of it makes me marvel at how Mother Nature works.

We skip Hidden Lake. It's a hike down. And what goes down must come up. We didn't want anything to do with that.

Shadow Lake is the least appealing of the five. The plant life in it makes it seem unapproachable.

It was Stony Ridge Lake that called to us. After traipsing across downed logs we came to the east side. The manmade rock wall that looks like a dam of sorts is not crossable. A slight breeze sends ripples across the lake. Sparkles of sunlight danced across the water. The clarity was stunning.

Perfect lunch boulders had us sprawled out as we soaked in the sun and scenery. The heat got the better of us and in the water we went. And I thought Lake Tahoe was cold. It was our secluded lake at least for one summer afternoon.

Twin Peaks:
2 Wilderness Areas On 1 Hike

Scenic: 6
Challenge: 6
Special note: Don't confuse this Twin Peaks with the one on the South Shore.
Getting there: From South Lake Tahoe, take Highway 89 north. Beyond Homewood and before Sunnyside in Tahoe City will be a sign for Kaspian Campground. Turn left. The road goes for about 7 miles. (Veer to the left and don't go straight on the dirt road.) At the end of the hill, the pavement turns to dirt. Go beyond the start for the trek to Ellis Peak. Parking for the trailhead will be on the right.

Variety is what the trail to Twin Peaks is all about. The terrain and views seem to change around each bend.

Rugged at times, lush at others. Granite and volcanic rock. Even in the fall there can be a few remaining wildflowers and a field of brittle dry mule's ear. Wide-open expanses, or closed in by towering pines. Lake Tahoe in the distance.

This West Shore hike in the Desolation and Granite Chief wilderness areas also at times follows the Tahoe Rim Trail and Pacific Crest Trail.

The Barker Pass trailhead is at 7,500 feet. The end point is at 8,878 feet. Most of the climb is gradual, so the elevation gain is not a deterrent. There is a small stretch that requires going down a bit after climbing. This is never ideal because it means on the return there will be an uphill segment.

Not far in there is a side trail to the right. This provides the first view of Lake Tahoe. While it would have been easy to stop there and call it a day, we were glad we didn't.

Not too much farther we came across a rock outcropping. The narrowness of it with a significant vertical drop is not the best place to be for someone with a fear of heights. A little handholding should get you through it. More spectacular views of Lake Tahoe are the reward.

It would have been possible to climb the rocks, but we didn't want to take the time. Plus, we had a dog with us.

The mostly single-track trail is well maintained. At times it is soft dirt, other times it's rocky. We were surprised to find water in a couple sections. This delighted AJ so she could stay hydrated without her people's assistance.

The water provides for lush vegetation like ferns.

We met a guy on the PCT headed south. We were happy to just be doing what we estimated was 6 miles total.

No bikes or motorized vehicles are allowed, though we could hear dirt bikes at the start of the trip on the road we came in on.

We stopped for lunch on the saddle. The vastness of Granite Chief Wilderness Area was mesmerizing. It looks like the forest goes on forever. It's easy to feel very small and insignificant, but also very appreciative to be able to embrace Mother Nature's raw beauty.

LAKE TAHOE TRAILS FOR ALL SEASONS

West Shore Snowshoes

"A snowflake is winter's butterfly."
— *Unknown*

Sugar Pine Point: Olympic History

Scenic: 5
Challenge: Varies
Special note: Dogs are not allowed. Trails are free, but it costs to park.
Getting there: From South Lake Tahoe, go north on Highway 89. Before hitting Tahoma, on the right will be a sign for the Ehrman Mansion. In less than one mile, make a left turn into the Sugar Pine Point Campground.

People with guns on cross country skis. That certainly set the tone for a unique day in the woods. Fortunately, they were shooting at electronic targets with laser rifles.

A sign saying "Olympic Heritage Event" made us wonder if we should turn around because we are nowhere near Olympic caliber athletes in any sport.

While snowshoeing is allowed at Sugar Pine Point State Park, the history here is rooted in the cross country skiing. This course was used for the 1960 Winter Olympics that were based at Squaw Valley. Now, competitions for non-Olympians are scheduled throughout the season, with biathlon events (where guns are used) part of the mix. Guided full moon snowshoe treks are offered on the lake side of the park.

At the shooting range, Holly Beatie was dispensing a wealth of information. She is well versed in the world of biathlon — which is the sport of cross country skiing and shooting. She moved to the North Shore of Lake Tahoe in the 1970s, but no women's biathlon teams existed so she competed with the men. It wasn't until 1980 that the U.S. developed a women's team. In 1984, Beatie was on the inaugural U.S.

biathlon team at the Women's World Championships in Chamonix, France, which won the bronze.

We left the competitors behind to strike out on the myriad trails in this state park along Lake Tahoe's West Shore. Steeped in history, interpretive signs along the way pointed out facts about the 1960 Olympics. At the entrance is a sign called the Tower of Nations, which is similar to what spectators at the 1960 Olympics were welcomed with.

When snowshoeing or walking anywhere near groomed cross country tracks, stay out of them. This is basic etiquette in the snow-sports world.

Fluorescent green lichen covered several trees. A few charred trees along the way were a reminder of the August 2007 Washoe Fire that destroyed five houses and burned about 15 acres. General Creek meanders between many of the trails, though it was not visible most of the time. However, at a few junctures we crossed it via a bridge.

Five distinct trails are listed as beginner, intermediate and beginner/intermediate. They range from 1.2 to 3.3 miles. Two are on the lake side; three on the west side of the highway. It's possible to do more than one. Grab a trail map at one of the park entrances.

North Shore/Truckee Hikes

"Adventure is worthwhile in itself."
— *Amelia Earhart*

5 Lakes: Visit Them All

Scenic: 7
Challenge: 5
Special note: Dogs are prohibited in parts of Granite Chief Wilderness from May 15-July 15 because of fawning season.
Getting there: From South Lake Tahoe, go north on Highway 89 to Tahoe City. At the traffic circle near Tahoe City take the second exit to stay on Highway 89/Lake Boulevard. At the next circle take the second exit onto Highway 89/West River Road. Turn left onto Alpine Meadows Road. (River Ranch is on the corner.) Drive 2 miles and the trailhead is on the right at the junction of the second Deer Park Drive.

Small ripples floated across the lake in the gentle breeze. A few ducks swam by to check out the four of us — five if you count AJ. She didn't faze them, even though she acted like they were intruding on our territory.

But where did all the people go?

There had been so many vehicles at the trailhead and several hikers along the way. Suddenly they were nowhere to be found. Not that we were complaining. A private lunch spot along a lake in the Granite Chief Wilderness on an August Sunday can be a rare experience. We embraced it.

Getting there was a bit of a climb at the start. The more than 900 feet of elevation gain is mostly at the beginning. It then levels off to where the ascent is hardly noticeable. Switchbacks are gradual so it doesn't feel like you are in a spiral. The decomposed granite proved trickier coming down because it was slick. Poles would have been nice.

The nearly 5-mile round trip hike starts at 6,660 feet. The five lakes are at 7,520 feet. Maps call this cluster of lakes 5 Lakes; they don't have individual names.

One rock outcropping looks like a cumulus cloud made of granite. Rounding another corner, there was a wall of granite that looked like it would be fun if you were into rock climbing, but scary if it were ski season.

With much of the hike being so exposed, we wondered why we started in late morning. Sweat was dripping without exertion. Fortunately, there were shady spots to rest in.

The trail starts on private land that separates Alpine Meadows and Palisades Tahoe ski resorts. Chairlifts from both resorts, as well as the terminuses, are visible from different vantage points. The base lodge for Alpine is a wide spot below us. A reminder of how much snow this slice of the Sierra gets is a sign at the trailhead telling people not to pick up unexploded avalanche shells.

Looking up at all the lifts proves just how sprawling Palisades Tahoe is. Plus, it's a reminder this is not true wilderness

The lakes, though, are in Granite Chief Wilderness.

There is a distinct fork in the trail as the landscape changes and the tree canopy becomes denser. Go left to make your way around to all five lakes. If you go straight, you get to what we called Lake 5.

The first two lakes are swampier, but still beautiful. They just don't beckon one to swim. The three other lakes seem more swimmable, with Lake 5 being where everyone else was in the water. No one was at Lake 3 or 4, which were the two lakes the four of us preferred.

Much of the area around the lakes is lush — almost tropical. An extensive trail network exists here, including the Pacific Crest Trail.

Palisades Tahoe: Breathtaking Wilderness

Scenic: 6
Challenge: 7
Special note: The Palisades Tahoe tram is free for hikers going down. Check to make sure it is operating.
Getting there: From South Lake Tahoe, go north on Highway 89. At the traffic circle near Tahoe City take the second exit to stay on Highway 89/Lake Boulevard. At the next circle take the second exit onto Highway 89/West River Road. Turn left into the entrance at Palisades Tahoe. (There's an Olympic torch and rings to let you know you are in the right place.) Follow this up to the ski area. Go to the end of Shirley Canyon Road; park on the side of the road.

Tumbling water splashing down from the mountains above; at times rippling across smooth rocks, other times in freefall.

No matter the winter snowfall, rivers and creeks in the greater Lake Tahoe area provide a scenic thrill for hikers in late spring or early summer.

Scampering up from the parking area the sound of rushing water filled the air. To our right was Washeshu Creek. It didn't take long before mini waterfalls came into view.

While the entire hike is not ideal for all ages, some of the most scenic areas are at the start of the trail. Young families have found this a good place to recreate.

Expansive "beaches" of granite called out as a potential sunbathing or lunch spot. We moved on because it was too early for a break.

The towering granite spires made us feel little. And we thought the pines were tall. The mountains on the North Shore seem bigger, certainly more jagged.

A soft dirt trail took us up. A few spots were muddy, but it was still early season.

Our goal was Shirley Canyon. We didn't make our goal. Sometimes taking a wrong turn can be a good thing. We ended up in another canyon.

What was so spectacular is we were all alone, embraced by Mother Nature. The trail was less defined there. We meandered along and through the manzanita as we headed into a canyon.

We crossed under the idle Silverado chairlift. The terrain was way too rugged to merely follow the lift up. Instead, we headed farther into the canyon, with the top of the tram to our right and in front of us.

We inched up along a snowfield, not wanting to walk in the middle of it for fear of breaking through into a creek.

Truly, it was breathtaking. I felt so small. I had this weird smile on face — being someplace new, where there was only the two of us, and where most hikers probably never venture.

Having skied here, I knew we were in for some dicey conditions if we pressed onward.

As we scampered out, in the distance we could hear loud talking. It turned out to be a smaller group of the 31 who were hiking together. (Mileage will vary based on where you turn around.)

What we should have done to get to Shirley Canyon was cross the creek. On a cursory glance it looked deep, so I picked the "wrong" trail. Going back, we saw it wasn't that big of a deal to cross. Just on the other side was a wonderful waterfall, skinny compared to the ones early on the trail. By this time, though, we were ready to find a different kind of watering hole.

From the trailhead it's 3 miles to Shirley Lake and another 2 miles to High Camp. Signage is better now so you should reach your destination.

Page Meadow: Multiple Options

Scenic: 6
Challenge: 4
Special note: Don't go off trail.
Getting there: From South Lake Tahoe, take Highway 89 north. Not too far after Sunnyside, turn left on Pine Street. Go right onto Tahoe Park Heights Drive. Then go right on Big Pine Drive. Go left on Silvertip Drive. The trailhead is at the end of Silvertip.

Something about meadows is mesmerizing. These vast grassy areas seem to appear out of nowhere. Such a contrast to all the conifers that dominate Tahoe hikes.

Page Meadow was not a disappointment; especially considering I had heard so much about this North Shore area that is part of the Tahoe Rim Trail.

Even on a summer weekend it can be uncrowded. In late summer a few wildflowers can still dot the terrain. The grasses were more golden than green, yet full of life. They didn't look dead or even dying. The actual meadow was more like fertile grasslands reminiscent of the Midwest. It was inviting in the sense that part of me wanted to run through it. I knew better. It seemed almost sacred. I didn't want to ruin the beauty for others.

Mountain bikers, too, kept to the trail that skirts around the perimeter of the meadow.

Even in late summer water was an issue in one spot. Fortunately, someone had laid down what looked like a homemade ladder that became our foot bridge across the boggy area. This might be the only area anyone would need or want hiking poles.

We were thankful for the fellow hiker who told us to look to our left for this crossing.

Signage is spotty. Multiple connector trails intersect with the main one. On the one hand this is good because it disperses users; it also means more options for accessing the meadow, as well as being able to lengthen the trek if so desired.

Starting out we were on what seemed like a road — wide enough to walk alongside someone. No aspect of this approximately 5-mile loop is steep. It's a gentle meander up and down, and around.

Palisades Tahoe: Guide Adds Substance

Scenic: 6
Challenge: 3
Special note: Guided hikes are seasonal; check Palisades Tahoe's website for info. Fee to ride tram.
Getting there: Take Highway 89 north from South Lake Tahoe. At the traffic circle near Tahoe City take the second exit to stay on Highway 89/Lake Boulevard. At the next circle take the second exit onto Highway 89/West River Road. Turn left on Olympic Valley Road.

Three golden eagles soared overhead. From this vantage point of more than 8,200 feet, it's already a bit like having a bird's-eye view.

Dave, our guide on this free hike out of Palisades Tahoe's High Camp, had us looking up at the peaks, down at the flowers, and out at the vast expanse of granite.

Like many who came for a winter to ski, Dave had been here for more than 20 winters. While his main job was working in mountain operations, on this particular day he was taking a group on an hour hike.

It was part history lesson as we learned about the humble beginnings of the ski resort that opened Thanksgiving Day 1949, to becoming the unexpected host of the 1960 Winter Olympics, to today's changes as evidenced by lifts being removed and others being installed.

Those Games were the first to be televised. "It was like a 12-day commercial for Squaw," Dave told us, using the name of the resort at the time. As Dave put it, this was back in the day when California was thought of as the land of oranges and surfing. It was not a skiing destination. It wasn't home to multiple winter Olympians.

It was the late Sandy Poulsen who helped name the legendary KT-22. It took her 22 kick turns to get down the mountain.

Wildflowers were out: yarrow, Indian paintbrush, mule's ear, pennyroyal, and fireweed. Dave picked some mountain sage leaves so we could discover it smells just like the spice.

Plenty of hiking opportunities abound. The later guided hike often entails going to Emigrant Peak (8,700 feet), but time did not allow for that on this first excursion. It's another 30 minutes from our turning-around point, which is at the Gold Coast chairlift.

Dave said from Emigrant Peak the San Francisco Bay Area peaks of Mount Diablo and Mount Tamalpais are visible on super clear days.

The Pacific Crest Trail goes through the area. The Granite Chief Wilderness Area has numerous trails. Hikers can even reach High Camp from the village area, which would mean an elevation gain of 2,000 feet.

While we didn't work up much of a sweat on this cool summer day, we still wanted to catch some rays by the pool and listen to the band. A bar at the pool supplies drinks, while just outside the gate is food at the café. The pool is an ideal setting to relax.

Mileage will be dependent on the guide. The hikes are designed to be do-able for most ability levels and ages.

Donner Lake: Turbulent Past

Scenic: 6
Challenge: 2
Special note: Take time for the nearby Donner Memorial State Park Visitor Center.
Getting there: From Lake Tahoe, head west on Interstate 80. Take the Donner Pass Road exit. (There is a sign saying Donner State Park.) Go left at the stop sign. The park is on the left. There is a fee to park. If entering off the road, there is a sign that says "East Beach access." Veer left for the trail, right for the beach.

A park named after the Donner Party should be visited in inclement weather. It's the best way to get a feel for what the 81-member wagon train went through in the winter of 1846-47.

Wind was blowing. The temperature was dropping. A mix of rain and snow drenched us. We were not as unprepared as the Donner Party, which lost 36 people on the trek across the Sierra, but we certainly weren't ready for the elements.

For some reason we pushed on.

Being at the ocean on a stormy day is something I've always enjoyed. This was a bit like that. While the waves were nowhere near ocean-like, they were strong enough to appreciate the force of Mother Nature.

Donner Memorial State Park does not have many places to hike, but there is a 2.5-mile interpretive trail that is in large part along the lake.

Interestingly, one of the interpretive signs talks about the seven-year drought that started in 1987. The frail lodgepole could not defend against the mountain pine beetle that thrived in the drought-weakened trees. Strong winds in the winter of 1994-95 blew many of the diseased trees to the ground.

While this area is known for the deadly, cannibalistic wagon train, it is also home to part of the original interstate system. Before Interstate 80 there was Highway 40. Signs are still in the area depicting Old Highway 40.

Before that, for a short time, it was Highway 37. It was part of the 3,000-mile Lincoln Highway that went from coast to coast.

Prior to automobiles, though, there was the train. On this particular day it was too overcast to see up to the tracks. Those who ski Sugar Bowl know the name Judah. Theodore Judah was an engineer who surveyed the first transcontinental railroad.

It was Charles Crocker, Mark Hopkins, Leland Stanford and Collis P. Huntington who formed the Central Pacific Railroad Company. Mostly it was Chinese workers who in two years built the tracks through the Sierra for these barons of industry who capitalized off what amounted to slave labor.

To this day Truckee has a train depot that takes travelers to points east and west.

The natural beauty and intriguing history make the lake and park a multi-dimensional visit no matter the weather or season.

East Shore Hikes

"I learn something every time I go into the mountains."

— *Michael Kennedy*

Marlette Lake: Abundance Of Fall Colors

Scenic: 7
Challenge: 7
Special note: This is a good hike even without fall colors.
Getting there: From the South Shore, take Highway 50 east. Either turn left onto Highway 28 and then park at Lake Tahoe State Park on the right for a fee; or pass that turn and at the summit park for free on the left. That lot can get full.

Autumn has such a distinct scent. You know it when you smell it.

All along the trail to Marlette Lake I kept taking deep breaths. While it is really death that is in the air, the power of it gave me energy.

Perhaps it's the power of nature to cycle through life and death with such relative ease that makes me jealous. We humans have such a difficult time with such monumental things like life and death. But nature, well, she seems to embrace each season.

Aspens really did seem to quake in the gentle breeze. Shimmering in the vibrant sun on this rather warm fall day, it was hard to know if the leaves were hanging on for dear life or trying to shake free to move on.

It was like a painter's palette — all those shades of green, yellow and orange decorating the landscape.

Temperatures, wind and moisture play a role in this leaf changing business. Just like figuring out the peak time for wildflowers, it can be hard to do with foliage. It's such a ritual on the East Coast that foliage is tracked for when best to see it. Even the National Weather Service has a color meter. Mostly it's aspens along the route to Marlette Lake, though this is not the only flora turning color.

This can be a popular trail in the fall, especially on weekends. Expect to see lots of people with their four-legged companions.

Those of us with cameras seemed to play a game of leapfrog with each other as we kept passing one another.

Instead of taking the North Canyon Trail, we took the Marlette Trail. It's narrower and is not open to mountain bikers. While we didn't see any horses along the way, we saw plenty of evidence they had been out.

We aren't sure how far we went. The sign starting the trail on the Spooner side says it's 3.75 miles to Marlette Lake. The sign at Marlette says it's 4.5 miles.

Snow Valley Peak: All About Views Of Lake Tahoe

Scenic: 7
Challenge: 7
Special note: The east side of Lake Tahoe is the place to hike in early season because the snow melts faster there.
Getting there: From South Lake Tahoe, take Highway 50 east to the top of Spooner Summit. Just past the turn off for Highway 28 is a small parking area on the left for the Tahoe Rim Trail. (You may feel like you're headed to Carson City because it's just over the crest.) Park, walk. Trail goes to the right for the peak, to the left for Spooner Lake. It's also possible to access the trail by parking at Spooner Lake, but it costs money.

One of the hazards of wanting to get some incredible views of Lake Tahoe is that it takes a bit of climbing. But those 2,000 feet of uphill to get to Snow Valley Peak are worth it.

Fortunately, it's not one of those grueling routes that make you think house cleaning would have been a better activity. But it isn't something parents with little kids are going to want to try.

The 6 miles (one way) are part of the much longer 165-mile Tahoe Rim Trail. Mount Rose would be the next exit point of the Tahoe Rim Trail. Sand Harbor isn't far away, but it's not visible from the part of the trail we're on.

Even though the four of us did an out and back, it's possible to do a circle by going down to North Canyon Road. This is the dirt road mountain bikers use to access the Flume Trail. It means having to circle around Spooner Lake at the end.

We started our morning at 7,146 feet at Spooner Summit. Snow Valley Peak is at 9,214 feet; the tallest mountain in Carson City. (Carson

it a city and a county all in one, with a small unpopulated swath of land that stretches into the Lake Tahoe Basin.)

Several times along the mostly soft dirt trail are signs saying "vista point" that lead hikers slightly off trail for views of Lake Tahoe and the Carson Valley. Seeing both at once is always such a contrast in what this area has to offer — the liquid blue alpine lake versus the barren high desert.

Camping in this area must be done in designated sites. Signs point the way. These are the rules of Nevada's Lake Tahoe State Park.

Up we went, passing beneath towering pines spaced so the terrain can be enjoyed without feeling closed in. Shrubs were close to the ground, including manzanita.

The sign says 1.5 miles more as we were about to begin the trek across the ridge. The four of us agreed it felt like a whole lot more than that. Lake Tahoe unfolded below us. This is one of those hikes where the size is so obvious. Often it doesn't look 22 miles long or 12 miles wide.

Directly across from us, the mouth of Emerald Bay opened up, with the peaks of Desolation Wilderness looming over her. From this vantage point it was obvious how Fallen Leaf Lake is at a higher elevation than Lake Tahoe. Marlette Lake was a short distance from us.

It's the views of Lake Tahoe that make this 12-mile round trip hike worth doing over again. The elevation gain is 2,493 feet.

There is no water, other than possible late snow melt, so be sure to take plenty for you and your four-legged companions.

Galena Creek Waterfall: Hidden Gem

Scenic: 7
Challenge: 6
Special note: Note the starting elevation.
Getting there: From South Lake Tahoe, go east on Highway 50. Go left onto Highway 28 at the top of Spooner Summit. At the roundabout in Incline, go right onto the Mount Rose Highway. Park at the top of the summit on the left. The trail starts to the left. The starting elevation is 8,911 feet — the highest year-round pass in the Sierra.

Waterfall season is usually a late spring ritual. Not so when there is a huge snowfall.

Taking advantage of a Sierra Club hike, I ventured out with a group to the Galena Creek waterfall in the Mount Rose Wilderness Area. What a treat. I didn't even know this 60-foot high waterfall existed until then.

In mid-September it was more like summer hiking.

Part of the hike is along the Tahoe Rim Trail. From there it's also possible to get to the summit of Mount Rose.

It didn't take long to reach expansive views of Lake Tahoe, along with the meadow that spans both sides of the highway. Winding around the south, part of Reno comes into view.

The guide points out Tamarack Lake to our right, which through the trees could easily be missed. Tamarack Peak (9,897 feet) is nearby, though Mount Rose (10,776 feet) is the most dominate feature as it looms large for much of the walk.

It's a single-track trail that at times was wide-open and other times closed in by the forest.

While beauty was everywhere, the waterfall really is what makes this hike so outstanding. Looking at the rocks, it was easy to imagine how thundering the water must have been in the summer. It made me want to return closer to peak flow.

In the other direction was a lush, verdant meadow fed by these waters.

To the waterfall it was 2.4 miles, a 557-foot elevation gain, and 328-foot elevation loss. Our guides took us a bit farther, through the meadow with its gentle creek and wildflowers still vibrant. This added about another mile to our trek.

It had been a while since I had hiked with a group of mostly strangers. On the one hand it's nice to meet others and be led, on the other hand the pace is inevitably slower, and dogs are less likely to be allowed off leash. Still, the Sierra Club is to be commended for offering these free hikes and allowing non-members to participate. All that's asked is a $1 donation toward the guides' first aide training.

TRT: Short Segment With Long Views

Scenic: 7
Challenge: 5
Special note: Spend the time to read about the history.
Getting there: From South Lake Tahoe, take Highway 50 east. At the top of Spooner Summit on the right before descending into Carson City is a parking lot. If the lot is full, there are also spaces on the highway.

If you think Spooner Summit is busy now, you really would not have liked traveling this route more than 100 years ago.

A dirt road and a railroad line were there in the late 1800s. This was a critical link between Placerville and Virginia City during the Comstock era. It was all about logging and silver in those days. Much of the wood harvested from the Lake Tahoe Basin was used to build the mines in Nevada.

Today, Spooner Summit the road — or Highway 50 — is the main path between South Shore and Carson City. The summit itself is the gateway to some spectacular hiking.

At the trailhead on the south side of the highway are numerous signs depicting the history of the area.

"In 1860, French-Canadian entrepreneur Michele E. Spooner acquired about 640 acres of land with the idea of starting up a sawmill, a shingle mill and a hotel. He named the area Spooner Station. Ten years and several business partners later, Spooner had acquired interest in flumes, a toll road, and other businesses, and controlled a total of 1,840 acres surrounding the summit that now bears his name," reads one sign.

Spooner sold his flumes and toll road in 1872 to Duane Bliss and H.M. Yerington.

It was President William McKinley who in 1899 created the Lake Tahoe Forest Reserve. This agency predated today's U.S. Forest Service. When that government body came into being in 1905, this land became part of the Forest Service.

The four-lane road was built in the 1950s.

A spectacular aspen grove marks the start of the trailhead. Yellows and oranges shimmer in the fall.

We had our choice of destinations: Genoa Peak Road 3 miles, Ridgetop Lake View 5 miles, Kingsbury Trailhead 12, Kingsbury Grade 14, or Tahoe City 102. These are all along a section of the 165-mile Tahoe Rim Trail. We did the 6-mile round trip to Genoa Peak Road.

A couple mountain bikers passed and there was proof equestrians had been out recently. Those who were hiking were bundled up to ward off the crisp chill in the air, which became more pronounced as an afternoon breeze picked up.

While the largest dose of fall colors is at the start of the hike, evidence of the changing seasons dots various spots along the way.

"It's a collision of seasons," is how Sue described the mountainside in the distance with the aspens and snow.

Various groves of Douglas fir made her want to pick out a Christmas tree right then and there. Many were not more than a Charlie Brown tree.

While we didn't make it to the ridge view, there are ridges and there are views. Some are outstanding vistas of Lake Tahoe. Being so high, they are also vast views.

Spooner Summit is at 7,150 feet and the hike is a gradual climb, with the steepest (and it's not real steep) section at the start. Briefly the colorful tree-lined Spooner Lake on the other side of the highway is visible.

The single-track trail is in great shape. Don't be fooled by the first road you come to. It's not Genoa, so you have not gone 3 miles.

Prey Meadows: A Descent Worth The Climb Out

Scenic: 7
Challenge: 5
Special note: It's all uphill on the way back.
Getting there: From South Lake Tahoe, take Highway 50 east. Turn left on Highway 28 toward Incline Village. Go about 2.3 miles, park on the left. There is a gate leading down. A trail will intersect with this one, take it to the left. If you go straight, you will hit Skunk Harbor.

It's always an interesting hike when you have to flag down a truck to ask where you are. We knew where we wanted to go. And we got there. We just didn't know where we were when we went a little farther. We were in Glenbrook.

We got there by going through Prey Meadows, which was our original plan.

I just figured we could get to Lake Tahoe through the meadow. I didn't realize there would be a subdivision in between the two — and a private one at that. We opted not to even try to deal with getting to the lake; partly because we didn't know if we'd be breaking some law, and partly because we had gone far enough for one day.

It was about 9.4 miles round trip from the starting point at Highway 28.

Fortunately, there was a creek running through the meadow so the dogs could cool off their bodies and lap up the water. Still, it was good we brought water for them because it was a warm day and we ended up going more miles than expected.

The lush green meadow is so incredibly vibrant. It looks like it would be wonderful to run through, maybe even bring a blanket for a picnic.

We stayed on the trail, though, which got a little buggy in early summer. I can only imagine how bad it would have been in the tall grass.

Tall conifers surround the meadow on all sides.

Clearly the trail was a road at one time. It was nice having it so wide; made it easy to have a conversation. This area of Nevada was once a bustling timber haven that provided wood for the mines in Virginia City during the silver rush in the late 1800s. There are remnants of the old railroad grade.

The one mountain biker we saw made us think we might want to revisit the area on two wheels.

Spooner Lake: Easy Saunter In The Woods

Scenic: 5
Challenge: 2
Special note: There is a fee to enter the state park.
Getting there: From the South Shore, go east on Highway 50. At the top of Spooner Summit, go left onto Highway 28. The state park is on the right and is well marked.

Tromping along the dirt at Spooner Lake this really was a walk and not a true hike.

While this is something anyone can do on their own, this state park in Nevada sometimes has free ranger-led excursions. These treks then become educational as well as scenic.

For those who don't have a guide, plenty of interpretive signs dot the landscape. Plus, there are ample benches to rest and be able to take it all in.

"Native Americans did a lot for us. They discovered medicinal uses in plants and food uses," Bill Champion, supervisor of Spooner-Cave Rock units of the state park, told one group along the 2.1-mile loop.

Stopped at one of the grinding rocks not far from the lake, Champion explained how the Washoe Indians would use the willows that grow along the shore for baskets and for pain medication, much like people today take aspirin.

Jay Howard, supervisor of Lake Tahoe Nevada State Park, used a catchy phrase to distinguish between pine cones — gentle Jeffrey, prickly ponderosa.

Spooner Lake got its name from Michele E. Spooner, a French-Canadian who with partner Simon Dubois acquired 640 acres for a ranch in the 1860s. During the Comstock, the land included a hotel, blacksmith shop and way station.

While the state of Nevada acquired the land in the 1960s, Spooner did not become part of the state park until 1981. About 12,500 acres are in backcountry, while about 1,500 acres are what most people visit at Spooner, Cave Rock or Sand Harbor. All three of these locations are part of Lake Tahoe Nevada State Park.

Spooner Lake is mostly fed with natural springs and snowmelt. It is nearly 20 feet at its deepest. With a Nevada fishing license, people may try to hook rainbow trout and other fish the lake is stocked with.

Today, it's mountain bikers who dominate the trails. About 75 percent of trail users are on two wheels, while hikers and equestrians are the other main users. In the winter, Spooner has cross country trails, with back country cabins available to rent. Concessionaires will ferry mountain bikers using the Flume Trail.

East Shore Snowshoes

"Even the strongest blizzards start with a single snowflake."

— *Sara Raasch*

Marlette Lake: Solitude Escape In Winter

Scenic: 7
Challenge: 8
Special note: Go early because of the shortened winter days.
Getting there: From South Lake Tahoe, take Highway 50 east. At the top of Spooner Summit, just beyond the Highway 28 junction, there is parking on the left. Trail starts there. Keep Spooner Lake to your left. The North Canyon Trail will eventually be on the right.

Sitting on the rocks I wished I were in a chair that spun around so I didn't have to get up to enjoy the 360-degree view of this slice of Sierra beauty.

On this particular day we had Marlette Lake to ourselves. In winter, this trail is practically deserted; the complete opposite of summer and fall when hikers and mountain bikers are out.

It was stunning, warm and relaxing, especially after trekking nearly 6 miles to get there. While we started out with the notion we would be snowshoeing, the hard pack conditions were such that hiking boots were all we needed for most of the trip. It was nice to have the snowshoes for the final descent to the lake, and then climbing out. Poles also made for easier trekking.

At times part of the trail will be groomed for cross country skiing. Snowmobilers will often lay down a path that makes shoeing/walking easier. Much of the trail is wide enough for at least two to walk side by side because this is North Canyon Road.

The bare aspens were like tall white, stick figures protruding from the snow.

Marlette's history is rich, dating back to the days when silver was mined in Nevada. The dam forming the lake was built in 1873. The height of it has been increased several times; it's now at 45 feet high. The lake is 45 feet deep.

While fishing at Marlette did not open until 2006, brook trout were introduced in the 1800s, Lahontan cutthroat trout in 1964, and rainbow trout in 1984.

The rock island where we stopped for lunch had a sign talking about some of the history, including the chimney that remains on Rocky Point. It's the last remnant of what was a cabin built by James Mather Leonard and Jessie Hobart Leonard in 1933. They owned Virginia City Water Company. Marlette Lake, which provides water to Virginia City, was part of the company's holdings. Before the couple built the cabin, the other area structures were a caretaker's cabin near the dam and a Nevada Fish and Game cabin. The caretaker's cabin was supposed to be taken down in the late 1960s, but instead crews mistakenly took down the Leonard cabin. In 2005, the chimney was restored. The informational sign was erected in 2014 on Jessie Leonard's 91st birthday.

The state bought the water system in 1963 from the Curtis Wright Corp., which had bought it from the Leonards. The Marlette Water System, which still provides water to Virginia City, Gold Hill, Silver City and part of Carson City, also includes Hobart Reservoir.

Skunk Harbor: Just The Name Stinks

Scenic: 7
Challenge: 5
Special note: All the work is on the return trip.
Getting there: From South Lake Tahoe, go east on Highway 50, up Spooner Summit. Turn left onto Highway 28. Parking is on the left in 2.4 miles. Nevada Department of Transportation clears the area so parking is not right on the highway.

Seclusion, mixed with vast views of Lake Tahoe is what the trek to Skunk Harbor is all about.

Sometimes there is no clear starting point because of all the snow. Some years it's a pretty steep first 15 feet before it flattens out. Fortunately, a snowmobiler had laid a track for us, as had other snowshoers and cross country skiers.

While I try not to go off a dirt trail for erosion reasons, with so much snow it was inviting at times to break trail, traipsing through the virgin white. Sometimes it was fluffy; other times it was crunchy.

No matter where one looked, it was a winter wonderland. It didn't take long for Lake Tahoe to come into view. The openness of the trail in many ways made me feel like I was much farther removed from civilization than I was.

Tracks led to a knoll that we scampered up to get what was a stunning view of much of the lake. It's unfortunate such a lovely place has such a smelly name.

If only it had been warmer. Warmth and snowshoeing in winter are often elusive. Lingering on the beach this time of year is much different than in summer — not so inviting. Ice hung from some of the rocks along the shore. About a foot-wide stretch of sand was exposed.

Remnants of Skunk Harbor's past were visible. While the U.S. Forest Service now owns this swath of land on the East Shore, that wasn't always the case. Stone buildings near the waterfront once belonged to George and Caroline Newhall. They used it as a second home for their San Francisco friends in the 1920s. George Whittell then became the land owner. He once owned most of the East Shore down to Zephyr Cove. Pilings for what once was a pier protrude from the water.

It's a gradual 1.5-mile descent from the highway to the beach. The uphill ascent doesn't feel so gradual. The elevation change is 560 feet.

Alpine County Hikes

"Mountains are earth's undecaying monuments."
— *Nathaniel Hawthorne*

Showers Lake: It Can Be Raining Flowers

Scenic: 8
Challenge: 7
Special note: It can be crowded on weekends, especially when wildflowers are out.
Getting there: From South Lake Tahoe, go west on Highway 50. In Meyers, be in the left lane in the roundabout, taking the second exit onto Highway 89. In Hope Valley, go right on Highway 88. Turn right on Schneiders Cow Camp Road. It is at the Caltrans maintenance station on the right near Caples Lake. Go behind the station and park at what looks like a trailhead.

Showers Lake is so idyllic that it is one of the more sought-after resting points for hikers on the Pacific Crest Trail.

The terrain is flat, which is ideal for pitching a tent. While the water is colder than Lake Tahoe, backpackers say it feels warm after swimming at lakes at higher elevations. Showers Lake is at 8,560 feet.

Kim and Susan arrived before us. A woman asked them if they minded nudity. Nope. And off she went for a skinny dip.

We hiked in with Lisa and Ken. She likes the start of the hike because the expansiveness, greenery and volcanic rock are not like the typical Tahoe trek.

There were plenty of wildflowers to gawk at. After a heavy snow year, flowers can reach 6-feet into the air. In a drought year or when it's warm early in the summer, expect the wildflower season to be less robust and short. Still, one drought year Kim counted 23 flowers plus a puffball, which is a fungus. She said it's edible but would only choose to do so if she had to.

The unusual monument plant, after it has flowered, leaves a tall green stalk that looks out of place in the Sierra. Some of the flowers along the way included: lupine, Indian paintbrush, bluebells, phlox, sulphur buckwheat, scarlet gilia, Alpine daisy, groundsel flower and larkspur.

From the top of the ridge we turned around to see the runs at Kirkwood Mountain Resort. In front of us and to the right was Meiss Meadow, which hadn't dried out yet. Meiss Lake is to the left and then Round Top Lake with its distinctive buttress. Lake Tahoe is to the far left.

Just below the ridge was a strip of snow that AJ lapped at to quench her thirst.

The descent into Showers Lake is a little steep. The rocks on the soft dirt make paying attention necessary. It's the one spot where poles would have been nice.

Boulders around the lake are perfect lunch and lounging spots. A fisherman had waded out to one of the rock islands in hopes of catching a more substantive meal. He didn't seem to be having much luck.

And while we had the trail to ourselves, the lake became crowded by the afternoon. Midweek would be the most tranquil time to visit.

There are multiple ways to reach Showers Lake. Deciding which route to take will depend on how much time you have, how far you want to go, and if you want a one-way or round-trip excursion. Going in from Echo Summit, you will be on the Tahoe Rim Trail part of the time. Starting at Big Meadow trailhead, the trek goes through Meiss Meadow. Carson Pass has a few connections that lead to Showers Lake. It will be about a 5-mile day from Schneiders Camp.

Winnemucca Lake: Bouquet Of Beauty

Scenic: 8
Challenge: 4
Special note: There is a fee to park.
Getting there: From South Lake Tahoe, take Highway 50 west. In Meyers, be in the left lane in the roundabout, taking the second exit onto Highway 89. When it comes to a T in Hope Valley, go right onto Highway 88. The trail starts at the top of Carson Pass. There is parking on the left, as well as restrooms. The Carson Ranger Station of the Eldorado National Forest is there.

It can be like a convention of wildflower enthusiasts along the trail to Winnemucca Lake. Everyone seems to have a camera. People bend over to inhale what scent these wonders of nature cast off. A certain excitement fills the air.

The best time to go all depends on the abundance of winter snow. Winter weather is also an indicator of how robust the bloom will be. July, though, is the month to plan for this excursion.

Normally a congested trail is exasperating. However, the abundance of natural beauty is so intoxicating the other trail users weren't bothersome.

Splashes of rich purple lupine are often everywhere, along with the bright yellow mule's ear.

This 1.8-mile trek to Winnemucca Lake in the Mokelumne Wilderness Area can seem to take forever if you continually stop to take pictures.

People were circling Frog's Lake, some lingering long enough to swim, though it's predominately small children who don't know they're allowed to say no to cold water. By the rock outcroppings at Frog's Lake the vegetation is different than on the route to Winnemucca.

It's wonderful when a botanist, like someone with the Nevada Native Plant Society, is leading a hike. Poach some information, like learning about penstemon, potentilla and green gentian.

Meandering on this trail that is full of adults, children and leashed dogs, were fields of Indian paintbrush and lupine. Wild irises poked above some of the other lush flowers. It's as though every color of the rainbow was represented in the various fields of flora.

Miners' lettuce dotted the trail; there was a time when mule's ear would be boiled and consumed.

Finally, at Winnemucca Lake we stopped to eat what we brought with us, not what we found along the trail. A few people were wading into the water. We didn't stay long — a thunderhead was almost directly over us. With all that exposed granite, you don't want to be there when the lightning starts.

Don't be surprised if you see someone walking up the trail with skis or a snowboard. Backcountry enthusiasts don't stop until that white stuff is all melted. Well into summer patches of snow often linger on Round Top, the mountain at the base of the lake.

Raymond Lake: Variety Of Terrain

Scenic: 7
Challenge: 6
Special note: Not all cars will make it to the trailhead.
Getting there: From South Lake Tahoe, take Highway 50 west. In Meyers, be in the left lane in the roundabout, taking the second exit onto Highway 89. Turn right onto Highway 88. Turn left on Blue Lakes Road. Turn left toward Tamarack Lake. At the fork, go right. Veer right again. There will be a big wide area to park before you get to Lower Sunset Lake. If you are down by that lake, turn around. Part of this is a dirt road. While four-wheel drive is not necessary, the road is not ideal for a typical passenger car. The trail is to the right where we parked. Not far up is a single-track trail to the left — take it. There is not a trail marker at the start or for this first left.

With each step, it seemed like the landscape was changing.

Smooth granite turned into coarse volcanic rock. Sandy footing became hard pack. Towering mountains and pines gave way to 360-degree views.

If this was anything like what the entire 2,650-mile Pacific Crest Trail is like, it might be something I would contemplate doing. But then again, considering how good the beer at the Jeep tasted and the hot tub at home felt, I'm pretty sure my adventures on the PCT will be limited to day trips.

Brenda and I started our trek on a weekday morning and never encountered another soul on the trail.

We began at an elevation of 6,461 feet. Our destination of Raymond Lake was at 8,972 feet. Brenda's GPS had the trip at 5.5 miles going out and 5.3 coming back. We're not sure how we lost those two-tenths of a mile on the return.

Distinct signs of autumn lined the trail early on as leaves were already a yellow-orange.

We got to an overlook with a marker that said we were at 8,000 feet. While the view is a bit like being on top off the world, clearly there are peaks around us that are much higher. The Nipple (9,340 feet) is an iconic landmark. Reynolds Peak is at 9,690 feet.

Looking down we saw a vast meadow – the one that is by Grover Hot Springs in the Markleeville area. Across the way, a strand of water flowed from the mountains. This is one of two waterfalls we saw on our hike.

Pleasant Valley Creek can be difficult to cross in the spring depending on the runoff. During wildflower season the flora can be exceptional.

At times the trail was narrow, with a steep descent to one side. It was a bit breathtaking for someone like me, with a little fear of heights. I would have turned around had I been on my own.

Going along we saw what appeared to be large granite rocks with a hue of light red and purple, as though Mother Nature had splashed them with pastel paint. An orange, rough, moss-like substance covered other rocks.

The only turn on the trail is clearly marked. One way keeps you on the PCT; the other goes to Raymond Lake. An additional three-quarters of a mile and we were at our destination.

At the lakeshore there were enough disintegrated rocks to make sitting comfortable.

We saw a couple at the far end of the lake who must have been camping. Permits are required for overnight stays, but not for day hikes.

Supposedly golden trout are in Raymond Lake, but we didn't see any.

The jagged spires that form Raymond Peak are 10,011-feet tall. It appears there are caves in the mountain. Some of the flat surfaces of the rock wall look like they could be a paradise for climbers.

It's a definite paradise for hikers.

ALPINE COUNTY/HIKES

Granite Lake: Mokelumne Wilderness Wonder

Scenic: 7
Challenge: 5
Special note: Don't let the campground chaos deter you.
Getting there: From South Lake Tahoe, take Highway 50 west. In Meyers, be in the left lane in the roundabout, taking the second exit onto Highway 89. At the T intersection, go right onto Highway 88. Blue Lakes Road will be on the left. Follow the road (it's long) and park near the Grouse Lake Trailhead. There is a trailhead sign.

Hiking is supposed to be about getting away from the masses and being immersed in nature. That's why the chaos of Blue Lakes Campground was a bit of a turnoff, and caused us to wonder why we were there.

Fortunately, the campers seemed to think the campground and immediate lakes provided enough entertainment.

Upper Blue Lake was being drawn down and Middle Creek Campground was closed to reduce the risk of flooding if an earthquake were to occur. Seismic analysis of Upper Blue Lake Dam has necessitated these actions by Pacific Gas & Electric Co., which has the rights to this body of water.

As soon as we got onto the trail near Upper Blue Lakes it was like we were in a different world. Civilization, so to speak, was completely behind us.

We took the advice of backpackers to walk across the earthen dam, then go down a little hill to hook up with the trail. This meant not having to cross the creek.

The superlatives ran off our tongues. None of us had been there before. "There" being the trail to Granite Lake. This is the Granite Lake in the Mokelumne Wilderness, not the one in Desolation Wilderness.

A pleasant surprise was the dazzling display of wildflowers not far from Granite Lake. I can only imagine what they might have looked like at their peak.

From the trail we could see the backside of Round Top. It's the highest peak in this wilderness area at 10,382 feet.

The trail is a gradual climb with about 700 feet total elevation gain. It meanders by a lake without a name, before taking a short, steeper climb toward our final destination.

In some places the trees were dense; in other locations the foliage was lush from the ample flow of water, while other areas had rock outcroppings.

Granite Lake is aptly named because it is essentially in a bowl surrounded by granite; it's not as rugged as some areas.

Several people were there with fishing poles. They were hoping to catch golden and Lahontan cutthroat trout.

While Granite Lake is hardly a secret, it was a special little gem that until then the three of us knew nothing about.

It's about 5 miles round trip.

Meiss Meadow: Full Of History

Scenic: 6
Challenge: 6
Special note: It is 2.7 miles from Big Meadows Trailhead to Round Lake, 2 miles from Round Lake to Meiss Meadow. It's another 2 miles to Showers Lake from the meadow.
Getting there: From South Lake Tahoe, take Highway 50 west. In Meyers, be in the left lane in the roundabout, taking the second exit onto Highway 89. The Big Meadows Trailhead parking is on the left about 4 miles from the intersection of highways 50 and 89. The trailhead is on the right side of the highway. There are a few wide spots to park on the highway.

A golden meadow stretched for what looked like miles. It was barren and beautiful at the same time. Stevens Peak (10,059 feet) and Red Lake Peak (10,063) are nearby. A cabin and barn are remnants of civilization from an era long gone. Meiss Meadow.

Besides being the starting point of the Upper Truckee River, this section of Alpine County was once bustling with cattle.

A couple women on horseback offered a glimpse of what this area might have been like a century ago. Hitching posts are still out front.

Water flowing in the river behind the house was good for the dogs that came along with their people.

The buildings were constructed by Louis Meiss (pronounced mice) who emigrated from Germany in the 1800s with his parents. Meiss bought 1,000 acres, which included what is now known as Meiss Meadow, in 1878. It was all about cattle grazing at that time.

In 1936 the land was sold to another family. In 1965 the U.S. Forest Service acquired the property. The structures are of historical significance.

Today it is a paradise for hikers. There are a few ways to get to Meiss Meadow — after all it is an intersection of the Pacific Crest and Tahoe Rim trails. For those on the PCT, they have 1,000 miles to get to Mexico or 1,400 more miles and they'll be in Canada. We started from Big Meadows Trailhead off Highway 89.

Signs of fall were evident from the start as aspens and other flora were turning shades of yellow.

Big Meadows never disappoints. It's like being in a bowl of beauty with 360-degree views of Sierra serenity.

The trail in front of us was a bit congested even though it was the off-season. Mountain bikers and horses share this trail with those on two legs. Numerous backpackers were headed home, most having stayed overnight at Dardanelles Lake. Once we got beyond the turn off for that lake, we saw few people. We headed toward Round Lake.

We don't fish, but reports are those with poles can find Lahontan cutthroat trout at Round Lake. We stopped briefly for a bite to eat and to let AJ have a swim. The chill in the air and slight breeze had us moving on soon.

The terrain after Round Lake changes from typical Tahoe pines to a more expansive openness, with varied foliage.

It felt a bit more like the Alps with the meadows at this elevation. Though at the same time, thoughts of "Little House on the Prairie" came to mind.

We stopped again at Meiss Meadow, specifically by the barn to enjoy the scenery. Then we walked a short way toward Carson Pass to see the golden grasses in that section of the meadow. It's almost like there was too much to see; you want to stay a little longer to make sure you capture it all in your mind. It was both peaceful and rugged.

ALPINE COUNTY/HIKES

Markleeville Waterfall: All About Relaxation

Scenic: 6
Challenge: 3
Special note: There is a fee to enter the state park.
Getting there: From South Lake Tahoe, go west on Highway 50. In Meyers, be in the left lane in the roundabout, taking the second exit onto Highway 89. In Hope Valley at the T intersection, go left onto Highway 88. Follow the signs to Markleeville, which means turning right on Highway 89. In Markleeville, turn right onto Montgomery Street, then a right onto Hot Springs Drive. Driving into Grover Hot Springs State Park, go to the end of the day use area. Start the hike by making a left at the gate.

The rushing water made hearing difficult unless one spoke in a loud voice. It was one of those times when listening to Mother Nature seemed like music that could never be replicated. Nothing on my playlist sounds as wonderful.

Opening my eyes, it was a sea of blue. The sky above seemed to be tickled by some of the distant pine trees. Leaves danced in the, oh-so-gentle breeze. The crystal-clear water made me want to lap it up as though I were a canine. Granite boulders of all sizes beckoned one to sit or lie upon them. Completely vertical, I didn't want to move. I was so incredibly relaxed.

All of this after just 1.5 miles. Bliss.

I wasn't the only one dipping my toes into the icy cold and ironically named Hot Springs Creek and her pools that sit above the magical falls.

Grover Springs State Park is best known for the hot springs that are 4 miles from the heart of the town of Markleeville. As the county seat for California's least populated county, Markleeville is a blip on the map.

The falls are an easy walk along mostly a wide path. Getting closer to the falls, the trail has several offshoots. Just listen to the roar of the tumbling falls to find them.

It's easily one of those places where you could spend a lazy afternoon.

Charity Valley:
A Gift For The Senses

Scenic: 5
Challenge: 7
Special note: There is a fee to enter the state park.
Getting there: From South Lake Tahoe, go west on Highway 50. In Meyers, be in the left lane in the roundabout, taking the second exit onto Highway 89. At the T intersection, go left onto Highway 88. Turn right on Highway 89 toward Markleeville. In Markleeville, turn right onto Montgomery Street, then right onto Hot Springs Drive. Driving into Grover Hot Springs State Park, go to the end of the day use area. Start the hike by making a left at the gate.

The park employee didn't exaggerate when she said the hike to Charity Valley is steep.

Markleeville is at an elevation of 5,500 feet; Grover is at 5,800 feet; we went to 7,267.

The soft, single-track trail was not gradual. It was vertical. Without the shade of the massive pines and cedars, it would have been unbearable in the middle of summer.

Surprisingly, it wasn't that far up for the evidence of the September 2008 Burnside Fire to show its blackened remains. Trees there are forever scarred.

A smattering of wildflowers decorated the landscape, bringing color to the forest floor — Indian paintbrush, lupine, tiger lilies and snow plants can be in abundance. Ferns were on the lower part of the trail.

Butterflies flitted about, oblivious to the only two people on the trail. Hawks soared overhead. A solitary deer stood still between the trees, making me wonder where her family was.

The trailhead had a warning about mountain lions. I didn't think twice about it until seeing some unfamiliar scat on the trail.

Up, up and away the trail goes, until it's above the tree line. Then, views of the valley below and beyond open up. They made the sweat and heat bearable.

Finally, it's decision time. Right for 2.5 miles to Burnside Lake, left into Charity Valley or a U-turn to complete an 8-mile day? The latter was the answer. The ridge we came to and the vistas along the way brought us views we are still talking about.

ALPINE COUNTY/HIKES

Curtz and Summit Lakes: Dry Lake Beds

Scenic: 3
Challenge: 1
Special note: Bring water.
Getting there: From South Lake Tahoe, go west on Highway 50. In Meyers, be in the left lane in the roundabout, taking the second exit onto Highway 89. Turn left onto Highway 88 at the T intersection. Turn right onto Highway 89 toward Markleeville. Turn left onto Airport Road. (If you pass Turtle Rock Park, turn around.) The trailhead is the first left. There is no sign.

Bring water because despite the destination being to a couple lakes, there is no water to be found.

Dust bowls. That's what Curtz and Summit lakes are. Lake is a bit of a misnomer. A ring outlines both. A muddy patch was at the center of them in June.

Multiple signs explain things about the land, wildlife and history of the area. One explains how it is not unusual by mid-summer for the lakebed to be dry. Some years it is dry before the calendar even says summer.

The nonprofit Alpine Trails Association built the 1.1-mile interpretive loop around Curtz Lake. These trails are in the Indian Creek Recreation Area. Indian Creek Reservoir does have water.

Rural and remote define Alpine County. The trails underline this. What's nice is that the trails are so close to Lake Tahoe, but provide such a different experience.

Pinyon pines dot the landscape, along with Jeffrey and ponderosa.

More volcanic rock than granite is prevalent. Signs say volcanic eruptions 10 million years ago created the rock mounds. Other rocks were strewn about as though it might have once been a lava field.

The views were varied: from the lakebeds to distant Sierra peaks with splotches of snow, to mounds of rock, to grassy areas.

Both lakes are easy hikes. Even in the middle of the day in late June the temperature wasn't that bad. The interpretive route is a mix of shade and sun, with the trek to Summit Lake much more exposed.

Alpine County Snowshoes

"If the path be beautiful,
let us not ask where it leads."

— *Anatole France*

Elephants Back: Climb Aboard For The Scenery

Scenic: 8
Challenge: 7
Special note: A sno-park permit is required between Nov. 1-May 30. They may be purchased online.
Getting there: From South Lake Tahoe, go west on Highway 50. In Meyers, be in the left lane in the roundabout, taking the second exit onto Highway 89. At the T in Hope Valley, go right on Highway 88. At the top of Carson Pass, park on the left. The trailhead is by the Carson Ranger District building.

It was one of those incredibly perfect Sierra days: the sun beaming down, the sky a deep blue with streaks of white clouds, not even a wisp of wind at the top, surrounded by nature's beauty in the company of friends. If only these moments could be bottled.

This is how Craig and his six women — me, Sue, Donna, Suzy, Carolyn and Trish — started one New Year's Day; with a snowshoe to the top of Elephants Back in the Mokelumne Wilderness.

We took our time. Donna's gadget recorded us being in the wilderness for about four hours; only two of which actually involved walking. We put in 4.61 miles, gained 1,168 feet in elevation, and went to 9,584 feet. Photo stops were a necessity, as was a leisurely lunch at the top.

One reason for choosing this excursion was knowing there would be more snow here than at lake level. Plus, much of the trail is exposed so there was less likelihood of ice being an issue. The trail starts off narrow, which meant we were single file. The snow was hard in this section, so the claws on the snowshoes were welcome. So were the poles for a better sense of balance.

It didn't take long for Elephants Back and Round Top Peak to show themselves. At one point, Frog Lake was on our left and Woods Lake on our right in the distance. Part of this is also a segment of the Pacific Crest Trail.

Plenty of people had been here before us. While it's nice not to break trail, there were too many trails at times. We knew the direction we should be headed and had plenty of daylight, so it was no big deal. It might be a bit disorienting for those who are unfamiliar with the area.

Pausing, we turned around and not too far in the distance was Caples Lake. From this perspective it looked large and completely covered in ice.

At the base of Elephants Back the snow was like sugar. While it was ideal for our purposes, it would likely pose an avalanche danger once more snow arrived. This consistency does not make for a good base.

It was not until we were part way up Elephants Back that we were able to see a frozen Winnemucca Lake at the base of Round Top. We took off our snowshoes to make it up the loose volcanic rock of Elephants Back. There was no way to snowshoe to the top. That didn't matter. The views at the top of Elephants Back are some of the best to be had in such a short distance, especially since the expanse of beauty spills forth in every direction.

On our way out we saw people headed to Round Top with the intention of skiing down.

Carson Pass: Ruggedness Mixed With Beauty

Scenic: 8
Challenge: 7
Special note: This requires at least two vehicles because it's a one-way trek.
Getting there: From South Lake Tahoe head west on Highway 50. In Meyers, be in the left lane in the roundabout, taking the second exit onto Highway 89. At the T intersection, turn right onto Highway 88. Go past the parking area atop Carson Pass. Start at Meiss Trailhead, which is on the right. Leave a car at the Caltrans maintenance station farther down Highway 88.

For 360 degrees it was a winter wonderland. It was like being in the middle of the Sierra with mountains as far as the eye could see. Distinguishable landmarks dotted the landscape — Elephants Back, the runs at Kirkwood Mountain Resort, Little Round Top, Round Top, Hawkins Peak and others. Meiss Meadow resembled a frozen lake; with one person saying the cabins looked like Monopoly board pieces. Caples Lake, covered in ice and snow, was uninviting. The view of sapphire-colored Lake Tahoe may have been what General John Fremont saw when he first laid eyes on this alpine wonder.

What a glorious way to welcome in the new year.

Five of us spent a morning on an incredible snowshoe in the Carson Pass-Kirkwood cross country ski area. Plenty of tracks could be seen, presumably mostly from backcountry skiers. For the most part we were breaking trail. We knew where we wanted to go, but there was no set trail to get us there. That added to the fun.

It was minus 7 degrees in Meyers as we drove through. At the trail's starting point it was 10 degrees and had warmed to 22 by the time we were done. What a thermometer would have read on the ridge, where the wind howled to the point it seemed to take our breath away, well, it's probably better we didn't know.

That wind whipped ice formations onto rocks in what looked like works of art, especially with the orange lichen nearby. At times the snow was so hard our snowshoes made no indentation, while at other times it was like floating on pillow-like powder. In other spots it was a crusty layer we punched through.

From the trailhead we headed nearly straight up and then to the left toward the ridge we knew we wanted to trek along. Had we continued, Little Round Top would have added at least another three miles to our journey. We opted to drop down into a bowl. At the bottom we hooked up with the groomed trails of Kirkwood Cross Country and Snowshoe Center before we made our way to the Caltrans maintenance station where we had left a vehicle.

In all, we went 6.55 miles. We started at 8,573 feet and reached a maximum elevation of 9,444 feet. With the up and down route, we gained a total of 1,654 feet in elevation and descended 2,267 feet.

Hope Valley:
60 Miles Of Designated Trails

Scenic: 4
Challenge: 5
Special note: Make a donation for trail use when the yurt is up.
Getting there: From South Lake Tahoe, take Highway 50 west. In Meyers, be in the left lane in the roundabout, taking the second exit onto Highway 89. Go over Luther Pass. At the four-way stop go straight toward the yurt. Park.

Two things about steadily climbing up are often true: a great view is usually the first reward, and the trip down is often a breeze. Both are true on this snowshoe in Hope Valley. This is one of those areas just outside the Lake Tahoe Basin that is worth visiting year round.

With more than 60 miles of marked trails, it has a variety of terrain to satisfy all levels of snowshoers and cross country skiers. Added bonuses include free parking and no trail fee. However, Hope Valley Outdoors gladly takes donations. After all, it takes a tremendous amount of work to keep up this outdoor playground on the Humboldt-Toiyabe National Forest.

As we climbed, the forest seemed to hug us. We forgot there was a highway close by.

Although Burnside Road is drivable for a bit in the summer, in the winter no tires are allowed across the snow. We seemed to have this oasis to ourselves. It wasn't until we headed back that we finally came across other people out playing.

We followed the signs toward Secret Meadow, even though it meant going downhill. As we meandered around in a loop, openings peaked out to Hope Valley below us. Seeing the field of snow made me wonder what this meadow must look like in the spring and summer. Are there wildflowers? Is it grassy? Would it make for a great lunch spot? Is it as peaceful during hiking season as it is in snowshoeing season?

Continuing on a bit, a smile crossed my face. I saw a swing in the distance. I love to swing; that gentle rocking back and forth. With snowshoes on, it made for an interesting dismount.

We continued on, circling back to the main road. We kept going up. A sign pointed to a vista. The Carson Range seemed to go on forever. Stevens Peak loomed tallest from this vantage point. Maps and research are not consistent with its elevation — some say close to 10,000 feet, while others have it topping that mark. The peak is named after J.M. Stevens, who was a supervisor in Alpine County and ran a stagecoach in Hope Valley in the 1860s.

Sitting on the granite boulder having a bite to eat I took in the scenery. It's sad to see the blackened trees charred from the 2008 Burnside Fire.

Signs along the various trails are abundant, but not obnoxiously so. Maps are often available in the yurt just in case. Mileage will be dependent on your route. Lessons, tours and equipment rentals are also available when the yurt is open, with opening day usually on the Winter Solstice in December. Dogs are allowed, but no trash service exists, so pack everything out. This is a great place to snowshoe and cross country ski.

LAKE TAHOE TRAILS FOR ALL SEASONS

Carson Valley/ Carson City/Reno Hikes

"In nature, nothing is perfect and yet everything is perfect."
— *Alice Walker*

Jones Creek Trails: Canyons Near Mount Rose

Scenic: 5
Challenge: 6
Special note: Maps available at visitor center.
Getting there: The scenic route from South Lake Tahoe: go east on Highway 50. Turn left on Highway 28 at the top of Spooner Summit. Turn right onto the Mount Rose Highway in Incline Village. There is a sign for the Jones Creek trail system on the left. This is well beyond Mount Rose Ski Resort. The trailhead is just past the visitor center. The less scenic route from South Lake Tahoe would be to drive to Carson City and then come up Mount Rose Highway from the other side.

AJ's birthday hike was no piece of cake.

At 12 (that's 84 in human years) she was much sprier than her much younger mommy. As if I needed a reminder. What was a 9.2-mile loop for the two-leggeds had to have been at least 1.5 times that amount for the dog. At that age she was like the Energizer Bunny — she just kept going and going and going.

This is what she lives for — being in the outdoors, romping in new terrain, sniffing all those delicious scents that never cross my olfactory senses, and quenching her thirst from pristine water flowing from higher elevations.

The Jones-Whites-Thomas creeks trail system could keep people entertained for days.

This loop had a little bit of everything. We went in a counter clockwise rotation based on the advice of visitor center staff. From the parking lot it is 0.6 miles to the start of the loop.

Plenty of pines loomed overhead, but it's not dense. It didn't take long before we were climbing. This provided spectacular views of far off mountains as well as parts of Reno. Behind us the slopes of Mount Rose were all covered in white.

A segment of this trail is open to mountain bikers. All were courteous to let us know they were approaching.

Farther along we came across some downed trees that required scrambling to get over. AJ, showing off her part Greyhound agility skills, leapt across the debris as though it were a fun obstacle course.

Plenty of water was running in the creeks so AJ didn't need any bottled water. She even trotted across logs to get to the other side. There were four stream crossings. The challenge to them depends on how much snow there would have been.

As we started a long trek west, we knew at some point we needed to head south to get back to our starting point. But we were in a canyon and the terrain to our left looked steep. We didn't really descend that much, did we? Won't there be some sort of cutoff to get us back without going up?

Up we went.

We made it to the top — again. More views, more picture taking. It's an easy descent, but by this time we were getting fatigued. AJ on the other hand looked like she could keep going, right until she curled up on the blanket in the back of the Jeep.

Genoa Falls: Water In The High Desert

Scenic: 5
Challenge: 5
Special note: Carson Valley Trails Association is a good resource for this area.
Getting there: From South Lake Tahoe, take Highway 50 east. Turn right onto Kingsbury Grade. Turn left on Foothill Road. Park near the Snowshoe Thompson statue, on the right in the town of Genoa. Trail is across the street, up Carson Street. Park on Carson Street or on Centennial Drive for out and back hikes.

Carson Valley is becoming a hiking mecca, with new trails being created all the time.

Seven people and two dogs were on the 8.2-mile Genoa Loop. It has about 2,500 feet of elevation gain, which seemed all to be at the get-go starting from Carson Street.

The entire route is single-track. More than one person complimented the trail builders.

Luckily, we all talk loud enough to allow for conversation with at least the person behind or in front of us.

It didn't take long for expansive views of the Carson Valley to unfold. The land below looked fertile.

There are spots along the way where the trail splits, but they meet up again at the original trail. Our guess is these were good passing opportunities for equestrians or mountain bikers. However, a sign at the start says the terrain is challenging and not recommended for horses or cyclists. We only saw other hikers and some runners on the trail.

A short section was shale. Most was hard-pack dirt. Portions were layered with pine needles. As it gets warmer and drier, this trail is likely to be dusty, and definitely hot in the summer. Even in the spring it can be rather warm, making one appreciative of the shade that there was.

While I'm not big on using poles, I was glad I had them for the 1,400-foot ascent, and especially for the descent. My footing slipped in a couple places and the poles kept me upright.

What surprised most of us was the abundance of water in various sections. This was perfect for the dogs.

Genoa Falls, which is about 12- to 15-feet high, was a delight to come across. It fell from a sheer rock face. Moss covered the lower rocks, while bamboo sprung up along the creek.

"Lush" was the word Rosemary used to describe some areas of the route. It's not a word usually associated with the Carson Valley.

We scampered through Genoa, Schoolhouse and Sierra canyons along this trek. While plenty of pine trees reminded us we were still in the Sierra, the terrain was still much different than being in the Lake Tahoe Basin.

Prison Hill: No Escaping Ruggedness

Scenic: 5
Challenge: 4
Special note: Bring water.
Getting there: From South Lake Tahoe, take Highway 50 east to Carson City. Turn left at the bottom of the hill onto Carson Street. Turn right on Clearview Drive. Go to the end. Signage is good.

We were held captive on our hike at Prison Hill, captivated by the beauty and number of trails we could explore.

It was a first for the three of us to explore this section of Carson City. There are so many trails in the Prison Hill Recreation Area and Silver Saddle Ranch that this won't be a one-time outing.

The openness (as in no trees) makes this area ideal to explore any time of year but summer. It would be blistering hot then. Hiking outside the Lake Tahoe Basin is perfect when there is snow on the ground there.

Even though we were in the capital city, at times it felt like we were in a remote location of the Silver State. The terrain is rugged and beautiful. Sage was the predominate plant protruding from the otherwise barren landscape.

At times the Sierra Mountains were in view, providing a snow-capped magic and complete contrast to where our hiking boots were leaving tracks.

Looking east it was more desolate. Trails — not sure if they were for hiking, four-wheeling, equestrians or biking — could be seen in the distance.

Where we were, a lone horsewoman passed us. People were scarce. That was one of the nice things about the hike — so few people on a weekend. Dogs being permitted was a bonus.

Yes, ample views showed the sprawl of Carson City, but there is so much beauty around that the development was not a distraction. On the north side, the prison for which the hill is named finally came into view.

This is where the annual Escape from Prison Hill Trail Race is conducted. Tombstone-looking rocks have "Escape Route" etched on them. Not knowing where we'd be escaping too, we kept on our pre-planned route.

We started on the north side of the West Loop, then hooked up with the North Loop. In all it was just less than 5 miles. The start is nearly straight up — no switchbacks. It gets easier from there. Poles would have been welcome coming down.

At the trailhead is a sign with a map and mileage of various trails that range from 0.7 miles to 12.7 miles.

Pine Nuts: A Drop In Elevation

Scenic: 4
Challenge: 3
Special note: The average passenger vehicle would be fine on these roads.
Getting there: The trailhead is about 30 miles from South Lake Tahoe. Easy access from Kingsbury Grade or Luther Pass depending on starting point. Once in Gardnerville, turn on Muller Parkway going east. (There is a 7-Eleven on the other side of the street.) At the roundabout, go right onto Pinenut Road. Turn left on Pinenut Road 2. At the Y, go right onto the gravel road. The trailhead is clearly marked a couple miles farther on the left.

In April, wildflowers are already out in the Pine Nuts, just east of Gardnerville. Red, yellow, purple and white dot the landscape at the start of the trail. Even though there was not an abundance of flora, compared to the trails of Tahoe in spring it was incredibly colorful.

The Pinyon Trail is part of the network maintained by the Carson Valley Trails Association on Bureau of Land Management property. This trek was 5 miles.

Starting at 5,700 feet, the highest point is only 6,060 feet. The single track was well maintained. Signage was outstanding. This was important because there are trails that cross the main route that the newcomer might opt to inadvertently take. Most of those trails are for dirt bikes and the like, while the main trail is for hikers, mountain bikers and equestrians.

Much of the trail was a loop. Even this was marked so you know when it starts.

As the sun came out, it was a spotlight illuminating the snow-covered Sierra and Carson ranges in the distance. Between the trail and mountains, it was either flat or rolling hills — most of it green and lush.

Pinyon pines (Nevada's state tree) and Utah juniper dominated the immediate landscape. These short trees would not provide much shade. This area would be hot and not ideal for hiking in the middle of summer.

What was a nice change compared to most places in the Lake Tahoe Basin is that dogs are allowed off leash. A sign at the trailhead says people should pick up after dogs and horses. Too bad the wording is facing people as they return to their vehicles. The equestrians AJ and I passed had left their messes for us to walk around.

An abundance of trails exists in this area. Most looked like they would be great for mountain bikers or all-terrain vehicles.

Fay-Luther Trails: Something For All Abilities

Scenic: 3
Challenge: 3
Special note: In the heart of summer it can be beyond hot.
Getting there: From the South Shore, take Kingsbury Grade to the Carson Valley. Turn right at the bottom of the hill on Foothill Road. Park at the second trailhead on the right for shorter loops. The first trailhead (Jobs Peak Ranch) provides longer treks.

The Carson Valley (4,476 feet) is a drop in elevation, which means terrain that is different than the Lake Tahoe Basin.

Sagebrush was everywhere. The long spindly bitterbrush protruded above other flora. A few of the rabbitbrush's yellow flowers were intact. Farther up Luther Creek, white alder, willow and Jeffrey pines filled the landscape.

This area is home to hummingbirds, Bullock's oriole, yellow warblers and the California toad.

Dogs are allowed on leash.

Starting out from the Fay-Luther Trailhead we checked out the map at the entrance. Myriad loops interconnect in a relatively small area. A flyer told us about the Carson Valley Trails Association — a nonprofit "working with partners to provide access to public lands through a recreational trail system for present and future generations to enjoy."

Appropriately named, the Sandy Trail led us from the parking area toward the mountains we just crossed. Not far in was a sign that pointed to California in the direction we headed, and back to Nevada where we parked. I thought nothing of the sign as we went by. It made sense to me.

What I had a hard time accepting until I saw multiple maps was that the sign was actually indicating it was the state line. Most of our hike was in California even though most of our drive was in Nevada. It just didn't seem right. But I think the Bureau of Land Management knows which state its land is in.

An interpretive loop guided us along. We were slow as we read most of the signs. It's an education about who the trail is named after. The Fay family started a ranch near Luther Creek in 1863, and in 1905 was the first family in the area to have electricity.

Luther Creek starts its migration to the Carson Valley from Jobs Peak. Today it is used by farmers and never reaches the Carson River.

Ira Luther, who the creek and Luther Pass are named after, settled in the area in the 1850s. He tried to get the Central Pacific Railroad to cross what is now Luther Pass. Luther is credited with naming Douglas County after Illinois Sen. Stephen Arnold Douglas.

We ventured off on the Grand View Loop, figuring out quickly how it got its name. Here on the western edge of the Great Basin and in the Carson Range views of the Carson Valley are vast, with the Pine Nut Mountains in the distance to the east.

A grove of Jeffrey pines filled the trail by the same name.

Had we not been taking pictures and reading the signs, we would have finished these 3 miles in no time. For the most part it's an easy hike. The trail gradually climbs at the start. Grand View is a bit steeper. But for anyone used to Tahoe, this is easy.

Carson River:
Flat, Wide-Open Trails

Scenic: 3
Challenge: 2
Special note: Good for just about anyone.
Getting there: From South Lake Tahoe, head east on Highway 50. Go right onto Kingsbury Grade. At the bottom, go left on Foothill Road. Turn right on Muller Lane. Turn left onto Highway 395. Turn right on Stephanie Way, then left on Heybourne Road. The trailhead is to the left and is well marked.

Meandering through grasses more than 6 feet high, mesmerized by sage bushes just as tall and with thick trunks, a brief oops where the trek went through slick mud, the Carson River wending its way through the valley as the snow covered Sierra peaks scratched the sky — all of this provided more reasons to be thankful.

To keep hiking in winter requires dropping in elevation. The Carson Valley Trails Association has been busy creating trails throughout the Minden-Gardnerville-Genoa area. This one, the Bentley Heritage Trail, is like being in the middle of nowhere, and yet so close to civilization.

We were so used to hiking in the Tahoe area that is was strange to have no elevation gain. A 1 percent grade is what you'll encounter.

With no trees, it seemed like you could see forever — which was wonderful.

While the network of trails here is 4.8 miles, what is great is hikers can easily make it shorter. This is because trail builders made several links from one side to the other. The other nice attribute was the off-shoots to the Carson River.

Our goal was to make a circle. We kind of did that.

While I was thinking the signage was wonderful, there were a couple incidents where we weren't quite sure where to go. The main obstacle was when we got to what I would call the end of the trail, before it curves around to head back; the arrows pointed in both directions. We thought we needed to go right to stick with our plan to go counter-clockwise. It turned out this was one of the spurs to the river and not the actual trail. After a muddy adventure near the water, we turned around and figured out our mistake.

We also weren't sure which direction to go at another junction. Instead of completing the circle, we wound up going across to the side we started on.

Neither of these hiccups was that big of a deal, but for first-timers a little more info besides an arrow would be nice. Things like "river," "trailhead," "eastern trail" would have kept us where we wanted to be. Still, we would all recommend this trail — just not in the summer or anytime it is hot. It is completely exposed, with zero shade. The river might provide some cooling off, though.

It was easy to see how high the river had been the previous spring based on the erosion along the banks and what had been deposited along the side.

A surprising find were some tiny clam shells along the shore, that to this non-scientist looked like the invasive clams found at Lake Tahoe.

Carson Valley Trails Association, with the Nature Conservancy, local Eagle Scouts, and the property owner built this hiking trail system. The association is good about replacing boardwalks ruined by spring flooding.

The biggest negative for me is that dogs are not allowed. This is because cattle could be in the area. Horses, bikes and motorized vehicles are also not permitted. But I'm thankful the private property owner agreed to the easement that allows the public onto these lands. The easement protects 4 miles of the Carson River, conserves wildlife habitat, safeguards more than 1,000 acres of floodplain, and encourages sustainable agricultural practices.

www.ingramcontent.com/pod-product-compliance
Lightning Source LLC
Chambersburg PA
CBHW030329100526
44592CB00010B/629